SEIZE THE DAY

My Autobiography

SEIZE THE DAY

My Autobiography

TANNI GREY-THOMPSON

with
Rick Broadbent

Hodder & Stoughton

Copyright © 2001 by Tanni Grey-Thompson

First published in Great Britain in 2001
by Hodder and Stoughton
A division of Hodder Headline

The right of Tanni Grey-Thompson to be identified as the Author of
the Work has been asserted by her in accordance with the
Copyright, Designs and Patents Act 1988.

2 4 6 8 10 9 7 5 3

A CIP catalogue record for this title is available from the British Library

ISBN 0 340 81971 5

Set in 11.25/16 pt Berling by
Rowland Phototypesetting Ltd,
Bury St Edmunds, Suffolk
Printed and bound in Great Britain by
Mackays of Chatham plc, Chatham, Kent

Hodder and Stoughton
A division of Hodder Headline
338 Euston Road
London NW1 3BH

This book is dedicated to my family, friends and supporters who have backed me at all times. They joined in the celebrations through my successes, but more importantly stood by me when sporting success seemed a long way away. They listened to me talking about training, competing, equipment, and never appeared to get too bored. They believed in me, taught me to 'aim high', and allowed me the time to be able to achieve.

Contents

Acknowledgements

I would particularly like to thank the following:

Rick Broadbent who sat through my ramblings, and put some order in to my life.

Martin Corck who encouraged me to believe I had a story that should be told and who is so much more than just an 'agent'.

Denise Harding and everyone at Creating Excellence who have had to read the manuscript more times than should have been necessary, and who have supported me through the last five years.

Roy Anthony, Dave Williams, and Jenni Banks who have stood beside numerous tracks in all weathers because of their love of the sport and the faith they have shown in me.

Photographic Acknowledgements

The author and publisher would like to thank the following for permission to reproduce photographs.

Allsport, Associated Press, BBC Television, Graham Bool Photography, David Boughton, Colorsport, Empics, News International/Chris Harris, Pearson Television, Popperfoto, Press Association, Times Newspapers/Andy Watts, Rik Tomlinson, Topham Picturepoint.

All other photographs are from private collections.

Chronology

Date of Birth   26 July 1969

1987   **International meeting, Vienna**
Represented Great Britain track team for the first time

1988   **Paralympics, Seoul, South Korea**
100m Fourth
400m Bronze medal

1990   **World Championships, Assen, Holland**
100m Silver medal
200m Silver medal
400m Bronze medal

Commonwealth Games, Auckland, demonstration event
800m Third

London Marathon, women's division
Fourth (2:49)

1991   **World Wheelchair Games, Stoke Mandeville, England**
100m Gold medal
200m Gold medal
400m Silver medal
Marathon Gold medal

Graduated from Loughborough University of Technology
with an honours degree in Politics and Social Administration

1992   **Melbourne International track meet, Australia**
200m World record (33.01)

Lake Sempach Marathon
First British woman to go under two hours (1:50.11)

London Marathon, women's division
First

Toronto Challenge, Canada
100m World record (17.76)
200m World record (31.04)
400m World record (1.03.00)
800m World record (2.05.59)

Olympic Games, Barcelona, Spain, demonstration event
800m personal best (1.55)

Paralympic Games, Barcelona, Spain
100m Gold medal and world record (17.55)
200m Gold medal (31.19)
400m Gold medal (59.2)
800m Gold medal (2.06.58)
All of the above were Paralympic records

Sunday Times Sportswoman of the Year

Royal Mail Best Female Performance of the Paralympics

BBC Wales/*Western Mail* Sports Personality of the Year

Variety Club Disabled Sportswoman of the Year

1993   **London Marathon, women's division**
Third

World Championship, Stuttgart, Germany, demonstration event
800m Bronze medal (2.01.01)

Swiss National Games
100m World record (17.36)
400m World record (58.66)

Inducted into the Welsh Sports Hall of Fame

Appeared on *A Question of Sport*

1994   **London Marathon, women's division**
First

World Athletics Championships, Berlin, Germany
100m Gold medal
200m Gold medal and world record (30.75)
400m Gold medal and world record (58.28)
800m Gold medal
10,000m Bronze medal

European Championships, Helsinki, Finland, demonstration event
800m Bronze medal

Awarded the MBE for services to sport

Sports Writers' Association Female Disabled Athlete of the Year

1995   **World Championship, Gothenburg, Sweden, demonstration event**
800m Fourth place

1996   **London Marathon, women's division**
First

Olympic Games, Atlanta, USA, demonstration event
800m Fourth

Paralympic Games, Atlanta, USA
100m Silver medal
200m Silver medal (world record in semi-final)

400m Silver medal
800m Gold medal and world record

1997 **London Marathon, women's division**
Second

World Championships, Athens, Greece, demonstration event
800m Third

Overall winner of the British Wheelchair Racing Association Road Racing Grand Prix

Appeared on *A Question of Sport*

Appeared on *This is Your Life*

1998 **Oz Day 10km, Australia**
Second

London Marathon, women's division
First

Lake Sempach Marathon
Personal best (1:49.57)

World Wheelchair Games, Birmingham, England
200m Gold medal
400m Silver medal
800m Silver medal

European Championships, Budapest, Hungary, demonstration event
800m Gold medal

2000 **London Marathon, women's division**
Second

Lake Sempach Marathon
Personal best (1:48.5)

Olympic Games, Sydney, Australia, demonstration event
800m Fourth

Paralympic Games, Sydney, Australia
100m Gold medal
200m Gold medal
400m Gold medal
800m Gold medal

Awarded OBE for services to sport
BBC Sports Personality of the Year, voted third
Winner of the Helen Rollason Award

2001   London Marathon, women's division
First

Currently the British record holder for the following:

100m	17.08	Atlanta
200m	29.77	Atlanta
400m	57.00	Gothenburg
800m	1.53.35	Gothenburg
1500m	3.35.15	Jona, Switzerland
5,000m	12.32.61	Jona, Switzerland
10,000m	25.39.6	Kirby, England
10km road	24.03	Mobile, California, USA
Half marathon	52.17	Great North Run

Prologue

The Ramp

'And in third place, Britain's best known Paralympian . . .'

That's me! Disbelief quickly gave way to an inane grin. Ever since I'd been a young girl, I'd dreamt of winning a BBC *Sports Personality of the Year* award and now that dream was a reality. But the issue that would dominate the papers the following morning was not the fact I'd become the first Paralympian to be honoured in such a way or the fulfilment of a lifelong ambition, but the simple lack of a ramp. An oversight by the BBC propelled disability sport into the headlines and ended up raising awareness in a way that any number of gold medals could never do.

It is traditional for the BBC award-winners to leave their seats and collect their trophies on the stage. But I quickly realised that there was nowhere for me to go. The only way I could have got on to the stage was by getting out of my wheelchair and crawling across the floor. I have no problem in doing that. You have to accept that, as a disabled person, you sometimes have to do things differently, but I knew that would embarrass people. So I sat there while Steve Redgrave and Denise Lewis, who came first and second, stood on the stage.

The lack of a ramp for me to join them did not bother me. I was just thrilled to get an award. No Paralympian had ever come close before and the most we had ever got in the past was a couple of quick film clips as they reviewed the year. It was only afterwards that I realised there was an issue. Kelly Holmes, the runner, whom I know, came up to me at the post-awards party and told me she had been trying to drum up support to march down to where I was sitting and lift me on to the stage. Then a few other members of the Olympic team came up and asked me why I wasn't on the stage. So did Kate Hoey, the Minister for Sport. Steve Redgrave and Matthew Pinsent admitted they had both considered how appropriate it would have been to carry me on to the stage. I was glad they didn't. It's not that I've got a problem with a couple of lads manhandling me but, if they had done that, there wouldn't have been the massive outcry that followed. Suddenly the ramp was a major issue. The BBC was flooded with complaints. *Points of View* had its biggest ever postbag that week and it made all the national papers.

I wasn't angry about the lack of a ramp at the time and I'm not angry now. It wasn't malicious on the part of the BBC. They just didn't think. I did an incredible number of interviews about it in the week or so afterwards and I said the same thing in each one. 'These things happen. It was an oversight, that's all.' The BBC thought they could get away with it but things had changed. Disabled athletes could no longer be marginalised and stuck away in a corner. That night at the BBC highlighted the shift in attitudes towards disabled sport in the aftermath of Sydney.

Afterwards, the BBC produced a thorough report detailing how they should treat disabled people. Now, when I reflect on what happened, I am so glad that there *wasn't* a ramp there. It was such a positive mistake. I got my letter of apology and I am absolutely convinced that the BBC will not make the same error again. But two years ago there would not have been the same reaction. It was exciting to see just how many people rang in to complain and the fact that a good proportion of them were non-disabled showed how much the Paralympics had moved on. Disability had been thrust into the spotlight and it was a huge boost for the overall picture as well as my own profile.

People expect me to be furious and bitter that my big night was marred, but I'm not. Instead, I was hugely encouraged that such a mundane thing could spark such an outcry. Winning the award and the furore that followed made me appreciate just how far I had come, but it had been a long, long road . . .

Chapter One

From Tiny Acorns

I'VE NEVER thought why me? I've never cried because I'm in a wheelchair and I've never felt bitter. This is just the way it is. People feel sorry for me and assume I've got a sad, tragic life because they don't look past the chair. But if it doesn't bother me why should it bother anyone else? One day, when I was little, I was sitting on the kitchen floor and my mum asked me what I thought about having spina bifida. I said, 'Well, if it wasn't me then it would be someone else. I've got it, there's nothing I can do about it, so I might as well get on with it.' That's always been my attitude.

I can't remember the day I got my first chair because it wasn't important. Some people might find that hard to understand, but the trouble is there is this perception that walking is good and not walking is bad. For me that's not true because being in a wheelchair has given me more mobility not less. It's different for the guy who falls off a ladder and breaks his back. He's been able to walk and, all of a sudden, he can't. He has had something taken away. That wasn't the case for me and it's never stopped me from doing anything I wanted to do.

Spina bifida is congenital. You are born with it. Technically, it is the non-union of one or more vertebral arches. It can also cause severe brain damage, spasticity and liver and kidney problems. My spina bifida was fairly mild but it wasn't in the best place. If it had been a bit lower down on my back I might have got away with walking for a lot longer. I also had spinal curvature and that caused more problems.

I was born at 1.25 a.m. on 26 July 1969 at Glossop Terrace Hospital in Cardiff. My mum, Sulwen, admits that if she'd known I was disabled beforehand she'd have had an abortion. She thinks it is wrong to knowingly bring a disabled child into the world because of the pressures it can put on a family. That was before she knew me. I wasn't Tanni then. I don't get worked up or angry about that because if I'd been aborted I wouldn't have known anything about it. My mum's view is her own personal one and doesn't worry me.

The doctor told my dad, Peter, that if they were down to have a spina bifida baby he should get down on his knees and thank God that I only had a mild form. The first thing Mum asked was, 'Will she be able to have children?' It was a bizarre question but the doctor said, 'I suppose so,' and Mum was fairly satisfied. She didn't really want to know too much because she would have worried herself sick and, anyway, all I had was a small lump on my back the size of half a boiled egg. The doctors would come and measure my head too, but we weren't sure why. Later we found out they were testing to see if I was getting hydrocephalus when fluid from the spine builds up in the brain and swells the head. It often occurs with spina bifida, but luckily I didn't get that. If Mum had known that's what they were doing she'd have been totally obsessed and never stopped measuring my head herself, so it was probably just as well.

I was in an incubator for a few days and then I came home. My parents had decided to call me Carys Davina, but that was soon to change. When I got home to our house in St Albans

Avenue in the Heath area of Cardiff, my sister, Sian, who is eighteen months older, saw me and said, 'She's tiny.' I think she'd been expecting someone her size. Tiny quickly became Tanni and that's what I've been ever since.

I'm often asked about the way I've grown up. Anyone who knows me will say I'm strong-willed, but that's because it's my personality, not because I grew up with spina bifida. Mum admits that she is glad that it was me who had it rather than Sian. She is not being cruel by saying that but Sian is a totally different personality. I can be bloody-minded, while Sian is quieter and more organised. She'll plan things months in advance and knows to within a penny what's in her bank account. I think Mum was right. She'd have had a lot harder time if it had been Sian who had spina bifida because I was the sort of kid who would have run away if I could. This way she had a chance of catching me.

Now I can appreciate that Mum and Dad had a lot to contend with when we were growing up, because Sian had health problems too. The tube going from the heart into the lungs hadn't disconnected, as it should have done at birth, so she had to have major heart surgery to stop blood pumping into her lungs. These days they can do it with keyhole surgery through the groin, but then they had to open up her chest. Sian also had problems with her walking. Initially, the people at the hospital thought it might be because she wore bulky nappies. Then they thought she might have an internal form of spina bifida. Eventually, they discovered she had been born with a dislocated hip. When she was two she had to go to hospital and was put in traction for six weeks. She had to stay in a frog plaster for eighteen months. The day after the plaster came off we went on holiday to New Quay, Cardigan. We hadn't been there long and we were messing around on the beach when Sian fell and broke her leg. So she was back in plaster again! The problems must have seemed never-ending for my parents.

Dad was working as an architect, so Mum was at home trying to deal with a young child not doing very much and me. It must have been difficult for her, but my parents didn't want me to be dependent. They are practical people. Their attitude was that if Sian could do something then so could I.

Sian and I had a lot of arguments, as sisters do, and, in the middle of one, I called her 'Pig'. That stuck too. As far as new names went, I think I got the better end of the deal! We were either extremely close or always arguing. I think that was down to our different temperaments. I had a very explosive temper and would fly off the handle quite easily. I would get very annoyed by little things but I'd have to needle Sian for a long time to force her to lose her temper. By the time she did, I'd have calmed down and so she would end up sulking. I remember one time Sian went missing when we were on holiday in New Quay. We were staying in a holiday flat and Mum started rushing round in a panic, making lots of noise and shouting for Sian. In the end we found her under the bed. She'd rolled under there and gone to sleep. I was three and remember not being bothered at all by the fact my sister had disappeared.

None of us knew too much about what was happening to me. We'd been told I'd got this thing called spina bifida but that was it. The hospital didn't explain what it was and what was going to happen to me. Nobody told me my walking was going to deteriorate and that I'd end up in a wheelchair. They weren't great at communication. When I got a pair of callipers I was really excited. I went to the hospital and they made me sit on a piece of brown paper as they drew round my legs. That was how they measured you for callipers. It seemed very basic. I went home and was thrilled because I could walk a bit better and wasn't wobbly. But that night I woke up and felt something wet on my leg. I pulled back the sheets, put the light on and saw all these horrible deep yellow blisters on my legs. One of them had burst. They were revolting. It turned out we should have washed the callipers beforehand but nobody had mentioned that. Mum and Dad always encouraged me to ask questions about what people were trying to do to me, but the doctors would come and see me, talk among themselves and the decision would be made.

As I grew, so did the lump on my back. My family called it my bump. I don't know why. By the time I was seven it was the size of a melon. To start with I was walking and running around, but as my bodyweight increased there was more pressure on my spine and my walking got worse. My ankles and knees got weaker and I couldn't stand up for very long. I stopped doing things gradually. First it was hard to walk long distances, then it was hard to walk up stairs. I don't remember waking up one day and thinking, I can't use my legs, but slowly things began to change.

My bump didn't cause me any problems unless I banged it and then I'd get these shooting pains running up my back to my head. I did that once when I knocked it coming down the stairs and just sat there at the bottom saying, 'Bloody bugger,' and, 'Bugger bump.' I was only two but my grandfather, who we called Dubby Jones for some reason, had taught me how to swear. The trouble was he'd chosen the wrong sister. If he'd taught Sian she would have been more sensible and realised when not to do it. I knew when I shouldn't but did anyway.

That was the way I was. To be honest, I could be a real cow

as a small child and I gave Mum a few hard times with my temper tantrums. I really embarrassed my parents in a restaurant once when we were on another holiday. There were a few well-to-do people in there and I insisted on opening my boiled egg myself and then shouting 'Bloody bugger' this and 'Bloody bugger' that. I was only four and ended up screaming the place down. They had to carry me out of there. I was a little monster.

When I was seven I had to have an exploratory operation so they could look at my bump. Mum stayed with me for as long as she could and the last thing I remember before they knocked me out is seeing her face through the little round window on the hospital theatre door. I was very scared and was crying as I looked at her and then they put a tube of smelly stuff under my nose and I went off. I was only meant to be down there for a short time but ended up being there for four hours. They found all sorts of nerves tangled up inside. There were bits of my spinal cord that had come out where the spina bifida was and the lump had formed around it. The surgeon cut away the fat and tucked the exposed spinal cord back into the spinal column. To put it simply, they took my bump off and pushed the other stuff back inside. My back was flatter as a result and the jolts and tingling sensation had gone. It might all sound quite gruesome but it was never a big deal to me, although I was always going back and forwards to hospital to visit the spina bifida clinics. I had to get my kidneys checked out because it's quite common for children with spina bifida to develop kidney and bladder problems. I can remember the doctors telling me I had spina bifida, but I didn't know what that meant and I wasn't bothered anyway. I've never been the sort of person who just sits there and thinks, oh dear, I can't do this and I can't do that. I'd much rather figure out a way that I can. I used to have a Cindy buggy which I'd pedal with my hands and then I had a skateboard which I'd sit on and propel with my hands. I didn't consider myself different from anyone else.

I went to the local primary school, Birchgrove, and loved it. My best friend there was a girl called Sue Roberts. We met on the second day and were best mates from then on. She was quite a lot taller than me and helped me around wherever I went. When I started having problems walking, she used to come around school with me, holding my hand to support me. How many young people would do that? She would also pick me up off the floor when I fell over. We sat next to each other for just about all our lessons.

When I started wearing callipers I had to use a rollator, which is a sort of walking frame with wheels on the front. It was a while before I learnt to walk with crutches. When I was at junior school, the rollator was fairly big compared to me, and to get to the toilets I had to manoeuvre past a couple of steps. Sue was always there to help me. She used to pick up the frame and then guide me up the steps – she always looked after me. She was probably a bit quieter than me but was the most amazing friend. I was really upset when I found out that I wouldn't be able to go to the same secondary school as her. Sue went to a mainstream school but I wasn't allowed to. We tried to keep in touch but it got harder as we got older.

There were two other girls, Nicola and Karen, who were good friends at junior school too and I made a lot more when I joined Brownies. I started going because Sue did, and had a brown dress, a beret (not the bobble hat that most wore) and a new belt. Dad bought me a penknife and a whistle and I proudly fastened them on to the belt. Brownies was great. Every Wednesday Mum would take me to the school hall near our house where it was held. I ended up being made a sixer which meant I was in charge of my own group. At the end of the night we used to all link our fingers and close our eyes so that we could say our prayers. You then had to squeeze your neighbours' little fingers to let them know we had to let go. Sometimes you'd end up with Chinese burns. You would see how much you could twist and squeeze without making a noise, otherwise Brown Owl would tell us off. Then we used to take it in turns to skip around a big plastic mushroom in the middle of the hall to sing our goodnight song. The only problem was, with my callipers, it was hard to skip around the mushroom – well, I couldn't skip at all.

Later on, I joined the Girls' Brigade, which was linked to the local church. Sian went too. It was there that I was teased about being disabled for the first time. One of the other girls called me 'Limpy Legs'. It didn't really upset me and I just shouted something rude back at her. I can honestly say I've only been teased about being disabled on one other occasion. That happened much later, when I was in comprehensive school, and a guy said to me, 'I wouldn't go out with anyone in a wheelchair.' My friend, Michaela Escott, got him by the throat, shoved him up against the wall and said, 'Don't worry, none of us would go out with you anyway.'

Most people treated me normally and my friends were great. On another occasion, Sue and I went round the houses near where we lived saying we were collecting money for the blind. I was on my skateboard and we only got about twenty pence, but Mum wasn't very happy and made us take it back. She knew we weren't really doing it for anyone else.

When I was growing up I had lots of treatment designed to help me stay on my feet. I also had ultraviolet sessions to try to heal the wounds I'd get because of the way I walked. Nothing seemed to work. My physiotherapy was meant to teach me how to do different things to help my walking, but I remember learning more from Sue than anyone else. If she did something, I wanted to do it too. That was a massive incentive. She climbed a tree once so I tried to do it. It was the same on the school climbing frame. Sue could get up it really quickly, but I could only get on to the second bar. I always wanted to climb higher. I tried using my arms as much as I could to pull myself up and Sue would always rescue me if I couldn't get any higher or got stuck.

Inevitably, there were a few accidents. Once, I was sitting on the radiator at home, looking out of the window watching Dad and Sian build a snowman in the garden. I'd lost the feeling in and around my knees by that point so I didn't feel the heat. My legs got really badly blistered. When we realised what had happened, Mum took me straight to the doctor's where she was practically accused of child abuse. Not having feeling in my legs could have its advantages, though. We used to go on holiday to Brixham and I remember crawling around on the rocks, thinking hey, this is great, I can't feel my legs. I can do anything I want. I wasn't thinking, oh, I've sliced my legs to pieces. It was just good that I could crawl anywhere.

My cuts and sores would take a long time to heal, though, because the paralysis meant I had poor circulation. I needed a lot of treatment and, in the end, the doctor let me have something called Debrisan. It was incredibly expensive, about £30 for a small tub. It looked like sugar. The doctor told me they used it on bomb victims in Northern Ireland. We had tried everything on my legs so this was the last hope. I remember getting out of bed one morning and thinking that my legs were healing well only to find the wounds had opened up again. I sat by the radiator crying and calling out for Mum. I was so annoyed. But the Debrisan made all the difference and my wounds healed in a matter of weeks. After that I got a lot more careful with my legs.

My mum and dad knew they had to let me do things even if they might have been worried. One thing I loved was riding. I started going to the Heath Cardiff Riding School for the Disabled when I was seven and it gave me a wonderful sense of freedom. The first time I went I was so amazed to be taller than everybody else. I'd never experienced this before. I learnt quite quickly and was helped by Penny and Nick, the two instructors. I used to ride the smaller ponies and, when I first started, somebody would lead me round and someone else would stand by my side to make sure I didn't fall off. I didn't want that and soon learnt to do it on my own. The school had been set up by Dina Cadogan and Professor Peter Gray, a paediatrician in Cardiff. Dina ran the Brownie troop that I went to and Peter Gray lived next door to Auntie Clode and Uncle Ivor, who were close friends of my parents. He thought it would do me good to ride and he was right. I remember the night when Nick decided I was now able to canter. I was riding Silver, a nippy pony who was relatively frisky compared to Rusty, one of the ponies I usually rode. Rusty was a fattish thing who looked like a Thelwell cartoon and loved Polos. He was a bit lazy. But as I cantered around on Silver, with Nick running alongside me, I felt like I was flying. I was going so fast it was incredible.

It was while I was at the riding school that something happened that opened my parents' eyes and made them realise that it would be self-defeating to mollycoddle me. I was about ten and there was a chance to go away on a riding holiday in Bridgend. I really wanted to go but Mum said she wasn't sure because I was still a bit young. Then another couple said they weren't letting their daughter go, even though she was in her late teens. The mother said, 'If she goes then she'll miss her bedtime story and cuddle.' That woke my mum up. I think she thought, oh my God, we're not going to still have her at that age, are we? We're not going to be reading her stories at eighteen? They realised they had to let me do things for myself and that wrapping me in cotton wool wouldn't do anyone any good. So I went on the holiday.

I think Mum thought it was sometimes best to be cruel to be kind. Once, when I was five, she left me in the local shopping centre to do some shopping unaided. She insisted that I managed on my own. I remember trying to get into Boots, but not being able to because I couldn't push the door. People kept walking past and looking down at me as I struggled on. Then a punk with this freaky haircut, all shaved at the sides and bright pink on top, came and started talking to me. He opened the door.

My friends were a bit protective of me but not overly so. They weren't rushing around doing things for me and we used to have some good laughs. One of my best friends was Jo Dutch. We used to play a joke on people which was probably a bit naughty. What we would do is go into town and find a bench. I'd get out of my chair and sit on the bench, while Jo got in and wheeled herself up and down the street. When she'd attracted everyone's attention, she would calmly get out of the chair and start walking. People were totally shocked. Some thought they'd witnessed a miracle. We just thought it was very funny.

I suppose some people might have been looking for miracles when I went on a trip to Lourdes with a group of disabled children and adults in 1981. I'm not religious and had to move

Sunday school classes because I got in trouble with my teacher there. All I said was, 'How do you know God's a man?'

'Because he is,' she said.

'And how do you know he's old,' I said.

'He just is.'

'But you don't know that for sure, do you?'

'Yes I do.'

'But you can't know he had a beard.'

I was just sceptical, but I don't think she appreciated me asking difficult questions and I was moved.

When I said I fancied going to France, Mum's reaction was, 'You don't even like cricket.' We had to explain that it was Lourdes and not Lord's we were talking about! Before we went we were told about the miraculous healing powers of Lourdes, but I just saw it as a trip away. I knew there was no cure for me so I had no ambitions to come away from the shrine walking. By the age of twelve I'd figured out that things were not going to change and that life was going to be lived in a wheelchair. I didn't have a problem with that.

It was great fun in France and there were so many groups from Cardiff that we had to wear yellow and brown bobble hats so we didn't get lost. When we got there, the priest who went with us asked if I'd like to go into the water. It was a cold day so I asked him how the water was. 'Freezing,' he said. 'I don't think I'll bother then,' I replied. So he sprinkled some water over me instead. He said it would have the same effect.

Of course, it made no difference. My walking was deteriorating and I seemed to be seeing more and more of my doctors. As I got older, I got stroppier and Mum and Dad made sure I had a lot more understanding of what was going on, but the doctors were awful at explaining things. They would throw all these

12

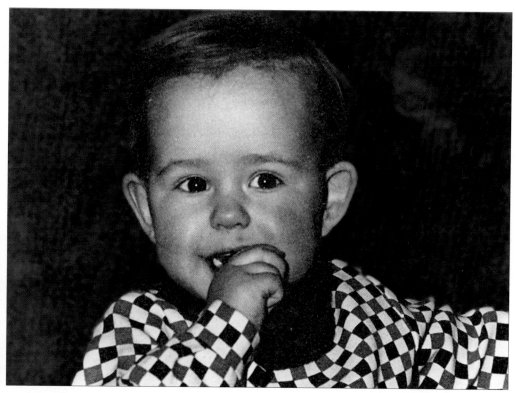

My first photocall.

Sisterly love . . . strictly for the cameras.

With Mum on our summer holiday in
Dartmouth – without my front teeth!

My first school photo – Sue Roberts is in the middle row, second from the right. I am in the centre of the same row.

First time away from home, at Brownie camp.

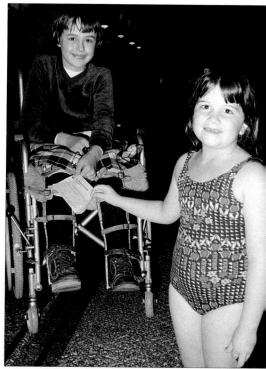

Wherever I went, the bobble hat came too!
Lourdes, Easter 1982.

One of my earliest public appearances, accepting
a cheque on behalf of Action Research.

Riding high on my friend Silver – horse riding was one of my early loves.

Roy Anthony – my first coach and early inspiration.

Lonely days in training at Loughborough.

Training in my first three-wheeled racing chair in Cardiff stadium.

'National Bill Day' – we all dressed up as one of my housemates, Bill Majowsky.

Dressed as Robin during Loughborough Rag Week.

Opening ceremony – Seoul. My first Paralympic Games.

Seoul – bronze medal in the 400m – Daniela Jutzeler was second.

You've been framed! Paul Brennan and I watching a re-run of the day's races in Seoul.

The comforts of the Olympic village. Three athletes, three beds, six chairs!

Porthcawl, 1989. My first marathon. Still one of the races I enjoyed the most in my career.

My first silver medal at a major championships, Assen, 1990.

Graduation day with all the family!

complicated medical terms at me, and I'd just sit there and go, 'Yeah, right.' I should have said, 'Sorry, but I haven't got a clue what you're on about, what you're doing to me and why you're doing it.' There were loads of kids at these clinics and I'd wait for five or six hours to be seen by a doctor, who would prod and poke me once or twice and then say, 'You're fine, off you go.' I used to think, what was all that about? It seemed a total waste of time.

The problem was the doctors were obsessed with me walking. Their attitude was I must stay on my feet for as long as possible. They wanted to keep me in callipers and then it was, 'You've got to learn to walk with crutches.' Some of the time I didn't mind walking, but by the time I was at secondary school I was getting fed up with it. The callipers went from my ankles to my thighs and I could only walk by swinging my legs about. I was never a girly girl, but they weren't particular attractive things and it was taking me a long time to get anywhere. I had to get up early in the morning and spend a long time putting them on. There was a lot of faffing around involved. It was hard for me to carry my schoolbag and my coat, and I couldn't run up and down the corridor at school like the other kids. Everything the doctors did was about keeping me on my feet when it should have been about finding the best way for me to be mobile.

My walking was becoming a problem but I decided to do a charity walk with my friends around the local Maindy Stadium in Cardiff. There were lots of us, but I was the one getting all the applause and there was a report about me in the local paper. I felt that was wrong. I've never been comfortable with the 'poor little cripple' reports and didn't see why I should be the centre of attention. But I suppose it was one of those occasions when I realised other people didn't think I was normal.

My problems with doctors continued. At one point they wanted to do an operation to make my legs the same length. Because of the paralysis, my legs haven't grown to the right length so I've got one that's half an inch shorter than the other. As a consequence I had to have a slightly built-up shoe on my calliper to make me walk straight. The plan was to cut a lump of bone out of one leg, slice open the other leg and stick it in there. That would entail pinning me up and putting me in traction for four months, all to make my legs the same length. I loved school and there was no way I was going to stay in bed for four months. I went to loads of appointments, I asked if the operation would do me any good and was told by a doctor, 'No, but your legs will be the same length.'

'But will I walk?'

'No, but your legs will be the same length.'

I thought, no way.

It was something my parents backed me up on. It was a family decision. There and then, we decided that we wouldn't do anything that wouldn't actually help me. And no way was I going to be a guinea pig. I am sure that a lot of kids with spina bifida before me were experimented on, but I wasn't going to be another. I didn't mind having essential operations, but that was the day we decided I wasn't going to have anything done that wasn't needed.

Chapter Two

Learning to Fight

BIRCHGROVE was a small school and I could get around it okay. Some days I wore callipers and some days I'd use my chair. It depended on what mood I was in. But when I went to comprehensive school it was a different story. The physios were still totally preoccupied with me walking. They'd tell me, 'We've got to get you walking around school.' I thought, well yeah, but it's a big place and I don't want to be spending twenty minutes struggling from one end to the other. When the bell sounded I wanted to run out at the same speed as the rest of my mates. I could do that if I was in a wheelchair.

Even getting into a secondary school was a fight and there was a long hard battle to get me into a mainstream school. That shows the prejudices some people have. Birchgrove was the local mainstream junior school and we assumed I'd follow Sian and Sue to the local mainstream high school at Llanishen. If only it had been that easy. At first the headmaster at Llanishen said I could go there but, when he found out I was in a wheelchair, he quickly changed his mind. He didn't want a disabled child in his school because he didn't know what he was getting. I remember the day we got the letter saying I couldn't go to Llanishen.

'Why can't I go, Mum?' I asked.

'They say the school's not very accessible,' Mum said.

'But why? I don't understand it.'

'Some people think you are different from them,' Mum replied.

'But the headmaster hasn't even seen me.'

'I know but some people are like that, Tanni.'

It didn't make any sense to me. Apart from one girl calling me 'Limpy Legs' and a few people looking at me strangely in the street, I'd never been treated differently. My headmaster at Birchgrove, Dewi Thomas, was a really sweet very gentle man and I thought the world of him. Because he'd said it was fine for me to be in his school, I assumed everyone would think like that. But suddenly I realised that I was being treated differently because I was in a wheelchair. I'd never experienced that before. I knew I was sitting at a different height from other people but that was as far as it went. I could do everything other people did. Now I realised some people didn't share my view and it was a shock.

The education authority said I couldn't go to Llanishen because it wasn't accessible and I needed special education. For a year my parents fought to get me into mainstream school. They argued that I didn't need special ed, as the jargon put it, just somewhere that was accessible. I was lucky that Dad is very politically aware. He got hold of the Warnock Report, which was the white paper for the 1981 Education Act, and read it through. He came to a little paragraph that said every child has the right to be educated in the environment that is best for their educational needs. I've still got the copy of the report at home. Dad started to write some very harsh letters to the people who mattered, pointing out what it said in the Warnock Report, but the saga dragged on. The education authority sent me to see psychologists and for IQ tests. Their attitude was you could be as thick as two short planks, but as long as you could walk through the school gates you had a right to be there. It was an incredible presumption. Later on I met plenty of kids who could have benefited from special education but didn't get it because they could walk. The education authority's attitude really annoyed me because they could have just looked at my schoolwork or listened to Mr Thomas who was hugely supportive.

For whatever reason they didn't want to do that and one day a man came to see me at school. He stood in the doorway watching me. Eventually, he came up to me and asked what I was doing. And that was how he decided whether I was suitable for mainstream education. I thought, you must be incredibly clever to be able to assess me by watching me from a doorway. Then I saw a psychologist who asked me lots of daft questions. How many days are there in a week? How many days in a year? Which way does the sun rise? I was ten and thinking, are you stupid or what? Why don't you look to see where I am in my class and then make a decision?

At the time disabled kids weren't in mainstream education, so the headmaster at Llanishen didn't see it as his responsibility. Legally it wasn't, but he just didn't want the hassle. He didn't have the desire to make the school accessible. I was devastated because I quickly understood that I wasn't going to be able to stay with Sue. The only place I could go to was Penarth where there was a special school called Erw'r Delyn next door to the mainstream school, St Cyres. I went with my parents to have a look at Erw'r Delyn. It was awful. There were kids of fifteen doing stuff like learning how to boil an egg and make a cup of tea. Mum was as upset as I was and looked at me when we left. 'Over our dead bodies are you going to that school,' she said.

The education authority didn't give in, though, and kept saying they needed to put me into a special school so they could assess me. My parents wouldn't allow it. They were even considering sending me away to boarding school, which they didn't want, but they were prepared to do anything to avoid having to put me into special ed. In the end we compromised. One day my parents got a letter from the education authority saying I could have a place at St Cyres but I'd have to go to Erw'r Delyn for dinners. I wasn't allowed to stay on site during lunch times. That was something else that didn't make any sense. Why couldn't I have lunch with my mates? I resented that but I pushed the rules as much as I could. I started pretending I needed extra help with my work so I could do lessons at St Cyres at dinner time and then I'd lie to the people at the special school by saying I was in detention. I made friends with another girl in a wheelchair called Lisa Jenkins who came from up the valleys, and we'd go back to St Cyres together after having lunch. Eventually, they changed the rules. There were fifteen other kids in wheelchairs and they realised that all of us wanted to stay at St Cyres. So they employed these young lads to carry us up and down the stairs, which was a bit strange, but it was much better than being in the special school. The teachers at St Cyres were okay. Sometimes I was a bit late for lessons because, with fifteen other wheelchairs, it could get a bit chaotic on the stairs and sometimes I'd be taken out of lessons early so there was time to get everyone up and down. When I go into schools now I often think how much better it is for disabled kids these days because they can go to their local school. Penarth was only nine miles away but it seemed like such a long way. I'm a naturally sociable person, but it meant I had no social life after school. I couldn't just pop around and see my friends because they were all in Penarth. That made it very hard.

*

When I was thirteen I had to have the second major operation of my life. My spinal curvature was becoming a problem and I had to have surgery to put it right. My doctor was David Jenkins and he was great because he had the ability to explain things at a level that a young teenager could understand. I had started to feel a lot of pain because, as my spine curved, it pulled the ribs round and distorted the shape of my body. It's a fairly common problem with spina bifida and the solution is to put a metal rod into the spine. I needed to have the operation; otherwise I might have become more paralysed. I didn't have a choice, but Mr Jenkins presented it to me in a way that made me think I did. The worst bit of having spina bifida was having to have the metal rod inserted because it was really painful. Afterwards, I had to wait for four hours between painkilling injections. For days I sat watching the clock and counting the minutes. As soon as the four hours were up I'd say, 'Get me some painkillers,' and the morphine injections were pretty cool. 'Wooaa, I'm doing great now, can't feel anything.'

They put the rod in at the top of my spine. Then they took a bone graft from my hips and wrapped that around the rod to get it to knit. I had two clips inserted at the base of my spine. That didn't really hurt, but it was very uncomfortable and I could feel it clicking. I've got some pretty impressive scars as a result of my surgery. I've got one about six inches long where I had my bump taken off. The one where they put the metal rod in goes the whole length of my back, and then I've got two big scars around my hips because they couldn't take enough bone from one hip so they did both. Once the rod was in they put me in a plaster cast jacket and I had to stay in that for six months. It went all the way from my hips up around my arms and my neck. Having that put on was frightening. They laid me on a bed and put traction around my hips and neck to get me as flat as they could. Then they put this gauze stuff round some foam and started taping me up with plaster of Paris. It was warm and soggy and I can vividly remember the smell. They actually taped over my head too so they could make sure the jacket was in the right position before cutting it off. The trouble was I didn't know they were going to do that. I thought, why are they taping over my head? They shouldn't be doing this. And then I thought daft things like my hair's going to grow underneath. It's going to look horrible.

It was a big relief when they cut if off, but it was gross having the jacket because it meant I couldn't have a bath for six months. The plaster around my neck got really rancid. I must have stunk. Nobody said anything, but they sprayed me a lot! One of the worst things I've had to endure was not being able to have a proper wash for such a long time.

I think the best thing about that operation was that it brought Sian and me closer together. When I was in hospital, Sian would come and see me every night straight from school and stay until 8 p.m. when my parents came and took her home. She had a Welsh exam around that point and didn't do very well in it. The teacher had a go at her at parents' evening, but my mum said, 'I'm not surprised she hasn't done so well, because she's spent the last three weeks and every weekend in hospital with her sister.' Sian hadn't told the teacher because that's the way she is, but we got on better after that.

I got quite defensive about her. Once a girl was being really mean to her in a shop. She was making fun of her mac. I started screaming at this girl. Five minutes later I was making fun of Sian myself, but that was my attitude. I could say what I liked about my sister but nobody else was allowed to say a word.

When I was young I wanted to be Sian because she seemed so much more grown up and organised than me. I looked up to her, although I never admitted that to her and I wouldn't say it to her face even now.

It was hard having the plaster cast jacket on because it meant I was totally dependent on my parents. I couldn't do anything. I was thirteen years old and Mum and Dad were having to transfer me into bed. They had to do everything for me. It affected other things too. Before I had the jacket I had been learning the piano. Despite being tone deaf, I had passed my grade five. Mum had played when she was small and we had a piano in the garage which Mum and Dad had turned into a playroom for Sian and me. We loved having a special room to keep all our stuff in, with two matching desks to work on. I liked playing the piano, but I had to stop when I couldn't see the keys because my neck was held rigid by the plaster cast jacket. Then Mum and Dad had to get rid of the piano because they moved my bed downstairs into the playroom. Because of the jacket I couldn't get up the stairs any more. Before the operation I would climb the stairs on my bottom and someone would help by lifting my legs, so I didn't drag them too much. That was impossible with the plaster cast jacket.

During that period I lost a huge amount of strength because I hadn't moved for six months. When I finally went to have the jacket removed, I asked the doctor if I'd be able to get back playing sport again. He said, 'Yes, straightaway.' But when they took the jacket off, my head just flopped down to one side. My neck muscles had become incredibly weak because I hadn't used them for so long. I sat there, my head down on one side, and said, 'Mum, there's something wrong.'

Before long I was in X-ray. I needed to hold my head up, but

I remember it wobbling back and forth. I literally had to hold on to it to keep it upright, which Mum and Sian found hysterically funny. About a week later I was able to sit up and slowly the strength of the muscles returned. Sian was delighted when I could finally have a bath. She thought it was great because she could have a laugh at all the dead skin. She sat there in the bath with me picking it all off.

When I had the jacket off, they told me it would be safer if I stopped riding. I had been excited about going again and I missed it, but I gradually moved on to other things. One of those things was sport. It was at school that I first started doing sport, although I suppose it was almost inevitable that I got into it. Sport was always on the television in our house. Mum is a huge sports fan and is completely biased towards Welsh rugby. Dad's more even-handed and wants to see a good game, but Mum just wants Wales to win and doesn't care how they do it. I used to watch a lot of rugby and remember being totally embarrassed at one Welsh international because she was screaming so much. She's Welsh-speaking and very patriotic. Dad was born in Cardiff, but we tease him about being English because his mother came from Birkenhead.

I don't remember a time when I wasn't involved in sport. Like most kids, I started off by doing stuff at junior school – rounders, netball and little PE lessons. When I moved up to St Cyres, I wasn't allowed to stay in mainstream school for PE. I was meant to go back to the special school but I didn't like it because I didn't know most of the kids. They were doing daft things like musical movement and pretending to be trees. I hated it. I wanted to do the good stuff.

The mainstream school had a swimming pool. One day when I was eleven I was watching the kids swim and the PE teacher,

Mrs Cogbill, saw me. I wasn't meant to be there and she was a very scary woman. I was constantly terrified of her. She looked at me carefully and then said, 'Have you got a swimming costume?'

'Yes,' I croaked.

'Well, bring it next week and get in the pool.'

So I started swimming a lot. I'd already learnt how to swim at junior school. Mr Thomas's attitude was that children had to learn to swim and there was never an issue of me not being allowed to go on the weekly trips to the pool. Mum would come with me to help me change and I remember the instructor, who always called me 'Chick', pushing me out into the water on the rescue pole and telling me to let go. I did and flailed around, doing a pretty pathetic doggy paddle, to get to the side. Eventually I did a length and remember sinking lower and lower in the water the further I went, but feeling fantastic when I'd done it.

It was difficult at secondary school because the sports I liked were things like tennis. At the time wheelchair tennis wasn't very well developed and it was hard to compete against non-disabled children. But then there was a sports day at the special school and I went to that. I didn't want to go because I didn't want to compete against other people in wheelchairs, but it got me off French, so I went. To my surprise I really enjoyed it. There was stuff like the 60 metres, cricket ball throwing and the slalom. We weren't allowed anything dangerous like discuses because we were from the special school, but it was a good day where you charged around and did lots of different things. I won a few medals, including the 60 metres. Dad's still got the certificates. After that I kept doing it more and more.

I don't remember making a conscious decision that I was going to do athletics and nothing else. I changed my mind about what I wanted to do every week. First I was going to be a dietitian, then a metallurgist, then a lawyer. I never thought I wouldn't be able to do anything because I was in a wheelchair and it annoys me when people assume you can't do things. People often come over to me and offer to help. I try and be polite but it can be irritating. At university there was a Chinese student who would always rush over and try to lift me out of the car, while I was fighting him off. The one time I can do with help is when I lose a wheel. When I park my car I have to get the wheels of my chair out first and, if I'm on a hill, they sometimes roll away. It always happens when it's raining, never when it's sunny. Once I was left sitting in the car thinking, someone will come along soon. Nobody did. It was teeming down with rain, but I had no choice but to get out and crawl through muck and puddles to get the wheel. And then, of course, somebody did turn up and I started swearing.

School ended up being a juggling act as I balanced my athletics with my studies and the usual teenage stuff. I used to spend a lot of weekends at Jo Dutch's house in Penarth. We'd go down to the sea front and hang out in a café called Rabioti's and think we were living it up. Jo was very sociable and had a lot of parties at her house. They were good fun and we'd make a cider punch and think we were really cool because we were drinking alcohol. We used to go to discos in town and, on another occasion, I remember Jo and me turning up for a fancy-dress party and finding out we were the only ones who'd bothered to get dressed up. It was fairly embarrassing so we sloped off and went for a knickerbocker glory in the Wimpey. They were happy days.

Jo, Michaela Escott, Lee Beckerleg and I used to hang around together and, as I got older, I found I had a lot of friends who were boys. I think that's because I was a bit of a tomboy. We'd all go to a club called the Marconi in Penarth and it was great because I could go dancing and nobody stared. I'd move my chair around and wiggle my arms. Everybody was very relaxed and just did their own thing. Until I passed my test, Mum used to be great about driving me to and fro and picking me up at all hours of the night. To be honest, I think she was happier knowing she could pick me up at a certain time in the morning rather than leaving me to my own devices.

I went out with a boy in the sixth form called Paul, but we weren't particularly bothered about boys at that age. I thought they were quite revolting really but I never got the impression that any lads wouldn't go out with me just because I was in a wheelchair. Most of my girlfriends didn't have boyfriends either. We just didn't get interested until we were about eighteen.

Most of my friends wanted to go on to higher education and I was no different. I'd known I wanted to go to university since I was eleven, although I kept changing my mind about what subject to do. I applied to East Anglia, Reading, Leeds, Swansea and Loughborough. I got offers from them all but decided Leeds was a bit far north and that, if I got ill, East Anglia was a bit far away from home. Sometimes you have to be realistic. On the other hand, Swansea was too close to home, which left Reading and Loughborough. I went to Loughborough, looked at all the sporting facilities and thought wow! I just fell in love with the place.

Back in the early 1980s, wheelchair athletics was just beginning to get bigger. The London Marathon was already on television and I remember watching Chris Hallam, the bad boy of wheelchair racing who lived just up the road, doing well. Chris was quite cocky and outspoken and was often in trouble with authority. He had the ability to wind people up. He also had quite garish clothes and made a real impression with his long beach-blond hair and leopardskin Lycra. Seeing him achieving things inspired me. I watched the television coverage in 1984 and thought, I could do that. Another moment that struck a chord with me was when I was fourteen and I saw the British men's basketball team. They all had Great Britain tracksuits and that impressed me. At that moment I thought, I want to compete for Britain. At the time I thought it would be in basketball, but the specific sport was forever changing. I'd go from 'I really, really want to do basketball' to 'I really, really want to do archery.' Then it would be something else. I competed in local and regional games in a variety of sports and then got selected to represent Wales at the Junior National Games at Stoke Mandeville in 1981. It was exciting being away from home for a weekend and I won a silver in the 100 metres and gold in the slalom. The slalom was a recognised event at the time, but thank goodness it isn't now. It involved turning, stopping, going up a ramp and was all a bit naff, although my time was a British record.

After that I kept going to the Nationals every year. In 1986 I can remember my teacher saying he didn't think I could win because I hadn't done much up to that point. I'd been to a competition two weeks before and won the 100 metres, but he said that was only because Sarnia Offside hadn't been there. I became good friends with Sarnia, who was the best girl in Wales at the time and one of the best in Britain. We had the odd falling out and would say we were never going to speak to each other again but we always made up. When my teacher said that about Sarnia, I thought, fair enough. But Sarnia was at Stoke Mandeville and I beat her and set a new British record. That was when I began to think, I can do this. I am quite good.

The following year I was named Junior Sports Personality of

the Year at the Rotary Welsh Sports Team Championship and then I won three golds and two silvers at the British Paraplegic Games in 1987. That year I also represented Britain at my first international meeting in Vienna. It meant we were away from home for a week, which was something at the time, and I knew most of the British team, so we had a lot of fun. There were a group of athletes about my age whom I met around that time and with whom I've remained friends, including Andy Hodge and Pat Bailey. My main memory of that trip is swapping vests with a girl who was a former Miss Japan. She'd broken her back in a car accident. She was absolutely stunning but was tiny, like a little doll. I was small, myself, but I couldn't get her vest on and it had been really baggy on her. That was the first time I swapped vests with an athlete and I've still got it at home. Vienna was also my first experience of the strange places athletics teams get to stay in. We ended up sleeping in dorms in a convent. It was a very nice convent but it seemed an odd choice. It was a sign of things to come. Last time we went to Switzerland we ended up in a Catholic respite home!

I've always liked training and began doing more and more. I like being out on the road on my own. You can think about stuff, get away from things and I like that sick feeling you get when you push yourself too hard. Like all athletes I also like moaning. I whinge all the time. Even when I was in Sydney for the Paralympics I was at it. Before my last race I told the coaches I'd had enough, that it was awful and I didn't want to be there. So Ian Campbell, one of the coaches from Staffordshire University, said, 'So if someone came along now and said they'd take you away from all this, would you go?'

'You must be joking.'

'Typical bloody athlete,' he said.

He was right, too. We all do it. You moan about not being fit, about being fit, having blisters, not having blisters. Whatever someone else has got you want and vice versa. I don't moan about being in a wheelchair but I moan like hell about being an athlete.

When I was starting to do quite well in the Nationals, I wrote a letter to Rookwood Paras, which was the sports club of the local spinal unit, asking if I could join. They agreed, so I went along and, a bit later on, I joined Bridgend Athletics Club, which was twenty-five miles away. That meant Mum and Dad would have to drive me up and down the motorway twice a week. My coach was Roy Anthony, who remained with me, on and off, until 1991. He had never coached a wheelchair athlete before but he didn't go easy on me. At one session he gave me some mobility exercises to do, which involved lying face down on the floor and bringing my shoulders back. It was designed to strengthen the spine, but I couldn't move more than an inch. My mum was watching and she said, 'It's a bit difficult, Roy, because she's got a steel rod fused into her spine.'

'Oh, my God!' he yelled. 'Why didn't you tell me, Tanni? I've been trying to turn you into a bloody S hook.'

When the track got really bad in the winter we would go and train in a multi-storey car park in the centre of town. When I think about the facilities we have now it makes me laugh, but whenever Roy said, 'Let's go to the car park,' we all thought, brilliant. We had a blast. Roy was a hugely dedicated coach, and he had a good understanding of teenaged girls because it can't have been easy with all those screaming hormones flying around. After the Sydney Paralympics I presented him with a surprise award from Bridgend Sports Council. I'd never known him lost for words but he was on that occasion and it was the closest I've come to crying in public. Roy's a lovely guy and deserved it because he gave up a huge amount of his time to help athletes like me.

We trained on grass at Bridgend, so when I saw Loughborough's modern track and heard about its sporting pedigree I had no doubts. Scores of famous athletes have been there, such as Seb Coe and Paula Radcliffe. It was 1987 and I'd started thinking seriously about the Paralympics. I knew that if I wanted to make it to Seoul the following year, then this was the best place to be. I got my A-level results and I was on my way. What I didn't know was that going to Loughborough would present a whole new range of problems.

Chapter Three

Korea Girl

S PORT has more than its fair share of fair-weather friends, which is perhaps unsurprising as the entire culture is based upon judging people by what they have achieved. To me that is rubbish. I compete for myself, not to please or impress anyone else. It is a selfish world. When I did well in the Barcelona Paralympics in 1992 I found it interesting and amusing how people's attitudes towards me changed. Suddenly, I was the flavour of the month. I was in. Then in Atlanta in 1996, the same people who had been fawning over me in Spain completely ignored me. The fair-weather friends were out in force again in Sydney. Some of the people on the team, who hadn't spoken to me in five years, were suddenly my best friends. 'How are you? Lovely to see you. Haven't seen you for such a long time.' They might have seen me the previous week, but they wouldn't have known. They were only interested in the medals table. When I came home from Australia, there was a long queue of them waiting to say goodbye to me at the airport. That would have been nice if they were doing it because I was Tanni, but they were doing it because I had four gold medals in my bag. It's the bit I hate. I'm lucky that, from a young age, I've had people around me who don't treat me any differently whether I win or lose. I've got my parents, my husband Ian and a group of faithful friends who accept me for who I am. The sycophants can fall off the ends of the earth for all I care. They're not real.

I find it hard to deal with the fact people react differently to me depending on how well I am doing in competition. It's different with the media because they have to be like that. They are only interested in success or, once you have been successful, complete disasters. That is what they are paid for. Personally, I've never been impressed by reputations. One of the questions that I am frequently asked is, 'Who was your idol when you were young?' but there was never anyone. I didn't have posters of pop bands or film stars on my bedroom walls when I was growing up. I always wanted to be me, getting out there and doing something rather than just dreaming about it. Steve Redgrave and I were talking about it at the Welsh Sports Personality of the Year awards after Sydney. We sat there for an hour signing autographs and I said to him, 'Can you believe these kids are prepared to queue for so long?' I said I'd never have done that and he was the same. It's lovely when people do that and the public have always been very kind towards me. But my philosophy is, like me for who I am, not for delivering medals.

At Loughborough you were judged solely by your performances and I found that hard. The athletics club was one of the biggest on campus and I remember turning up to the track for the first time and not being able to believe my eyes. It was a sea of Great Britain vests. There must have been 200 people and I remember just looking around and being unable to believe the size of the club. It was daunting and off-putting but I also saw it as a challenge.

Athletics can be a lonely sport because it is all about who is better than whom. As a result there can be some edginess and even bitchiness between athletes, especially leading up to selection, where you are competing against each other for places. Alternatively, there can be a camaraderie and support from being with a squad of athletes who are all on the same mission. That was the spirit I had known at Bridgend. When the time came to move to Loughborough I wasn't totally prepared for the new experience.

I'd been dreaming about studying at Loughborough ever since visiting the place. I had seen the list of illustrious former students who had made it in the world of athletics and thought this was where I belonged. I drove up to campus the day before the other freshers arrived because Max, my hall warden, thought it would be useful to get settled in before the chaos of parents and students arriving. I was housed in a specially adapted bungalow, along with Georgina, Fraser, Simon and Bill, some other first years. We were affiliated to the Towers hall of residence, two ugly high-rise blocks linked by stairways, but it was hard to get around at first because there were so many steps everywhere. The Towers dining hall and bar were inaccessible and it was easy to feel cut off being stuck in a bungalow 200 yards away from the main hall of residence.

I was nervous and excited about going to university, but the first week was daunting, not knowing anyone and trying to find my way around this huge campus. Luckily, I met a group of people early on with whom I remained friends throughout my time there. My closest friend was Nikki, a Londoner studying civil engineering. We met at the freshers' dinner. Nikki was quite strong and she would have no qualms about carrying me up and down the stairs, which was just as well as most of my friends were on the seventh, eleventh and thirteenth floors. There were 300 or so people in Towers so there was always someone around to pick up my chair and throw it after me. There were also a couple of strong blokes who would carry me about and my friends would lift me up to the bar. It wasn't a problem. A few people were a bit stand-offish, but that was most likely because they had never met anyone who was a wheelchair-user before and were not sure what to expect.

We had some good laughs and played a joke on Bill one day. He was a bit older than the rest of us and had come back to study after working as a nurse. He was fairly short, a bit rotund and balding on top. He always wore a red jumper and had little round glasses. One day we all got dressed up as Bill. We bought bald caps from a joke shop and glued bits of hair to the side. We stuffed pillows up our red jumpers and hid in the toilets while someone looked out for him. Eventually, he came by and we all followed him into the dining hall. When he twigged he was quite shocked but, fortunately, he thought it was funny. Bill was a nice bloke and I kept in touch with him on and off after we'd left uni.

Most of my friendships were made in Towers, not in the athletics club, and not particularly on my course. I had applied to study history but the department contacted me before term started saying that they were closing the course down and I must choose another subject if I still wanted to go there. It took a while to decide whether my wish to study history outweighed what I thought about Loughborough. I contacted the other universities that had offered me a place and they all said they were happy to renew their offers if I wanted to go there. In the end I decided I would have more opportunities by going to Loughborough and plumped for politics because I thought that it was the closest subject to history. It's fair to say that I was not the best politics student they had ever had and I was one of the few people on the course without any strong political leanings. I was interested in the subject and am very interested in the politics of sport today, but that interest was not fuelled by an overwhelming desire to go and join any political party. Most of the other people on my course seemed keen to go into politics in some form and some were hell bent on getting to Westminster – I had no ambitions in that area whatsoever.

I didn't have a single friend in the athletics club. I didn't like training with them and it was not made any easier for me by the fact that some of the training venues were not very accessible. Although there was a ramp leading down to the track, the gate at the top was always locked and so when I wanted to go training, I had to call security so they could come and open it. I was probably quite naive at the time as well. One coach suggested to me, 'Maybe it would be better for you to train on the track at a different time so that the runners won't get in your way.' I said, 'No, I'll be fine,' but then I realised what he was actually saying to me. It wasn't his fault because that sort of attitude was a product of the time. There were no other wheelchair-users at Loughborough and very few disabled people were going through higher education. Disability sport didn't have a very high profile and although the wheelchair race at the London Marathon received fairly good coverage, that was all the media attention we received. People didn't know whether the times I was doing on the track were good or bad because the only comparison they had was with the times of the non-disabled runners. I shouldn't have expected anything else, but I'd come from a big friendly club and that made it quite hard. Nobody believed the girl in the wheelchair could be an athlete.

And then there were the initiation dinners. They were the norm for every sporting society at the university and, like everyone else, I joined in. We had a dinner and then it was a case of playing icebreaker games and having a few more drinks. The hardest part for me was that I could get drunk very easily, usually on less than half a pint. These days it is even less! I went to the athletics club's initiation dinner but didn't enjoy it. There were a lot of daft games but I didn't feel a part of it. I couldn't hop around on one leg and didn't see the point in getting drunk and trying to hurdle barbed-wire fences. They tried to adapt the games but that made it worse. Being non-disabled can be a no-win situation when it comes to dealing with wheelchair-users. I know people sometimes feel awkward and don't know how they should react. But I don't feel the need for other people to be on the same level as me and find the sudden dash to find a seat to match my height slightly funny, although if it makes people feel better then that is fine. On the other side of the coin, trying to chat socially in a noisy room of a couple of hundred people when you are only three foot tall isn't easy. I am quite outgoing and thrive when I am around my close friends and family but, even after years of public speaking and engagements, I don't enjoy walking into a room of complete strangers. Who does? And it was worse when I was a teenager starting out at university. I felt I was trying to fit into a club that didn't really want me.

The problem with track access made me go out training on the road and also made me find other more appropriate groups to train with. Training with the athletics club was not helping me. The emphasis was on legs which was not a lot of use when mine didn't work. I flitted around the sessions, climbing ropes and doing push-ups and sit-ups, but that was about all I could do. It was hard to fit in. After a year I figured out that I had to try something else.

One night I'd come back from circuit training and was having a coffee with Nikki and her friend Carl, doing my usual moaning routine about the athletics club. I said I needed to find a new way of circuit training because I was getting bored with doing the same three or four exercises. Carl was into mountaineering and he said, 'Why don't you come and join our club instead?' I thought okay, why not? That was a turning point. I went along and I knew Carl and a couple of the other guys, which got me over the first hurdle of not knowing anyone. It was a totally different environment from the athletics club. There were only about twenty people there and the focus was on the upper body which meant I could do most of the exercises. And if there was something that I couldn't do we'd find a way I could. They were more under-standing and open-minded, but I think that is the nature of the sport and the type of people it attracts. Their attitude was, 'Crikey, she can climb to the top of that rope without using her legs,' whereas in athletics it was, 'Why is she taking so long to climb that rope?' The mountaineers knew how hard it was for me and there wasn't that same competitive element.

I think I am naturally competitive, but that does not apply to every situation and that is why I train with different groups of people. I very rarely train with other female athletes because of the danger of trying to compete against them. It is very easy to fall into race mode at the wrong time. My strength is in knowing exactly what I have to do to reap the most benefit from my training. Athletes are obsessed with their rankings and times, but I can't be bothered with any of that in training. Don't get me wrong. I take training very seriously, but you do the business when it matters, not in training when you are just scoring points off each other. Throughout my career I have learnt that there is a fine line between training hard and over-training. The mountaineering club was refreshing for me. Nobody cared about who was faster than whom; they just wanted to push themselves to the limit. We'd come out of sessions absolutely exhausted, aching so much that it was hard to move the next day. It was fun without the hierarchy.

A training session at the mountaineering club one night turned out to have far-reaching consequences for me. It was a normal hard training session. I remember Carl saying, 'You're really tired, Tanni. Don't do the last rope climb.' I should have listened to him. Instead, I just said, 'I'm fine, Carl.' But on the way up I knew that I wasn't going to make it to the top and that I needed enough strength to get back down. As I started my descent I suddenly felt an excruciating pain in my stomach. I'd pulled my stomach muscles and slipped from the rope. I remember sitting on the floor for a while, feeling these shooting pains in my back. I figured that it was just the way I'd fallen and that my spine had taken a knock. Carl told me to rest on the floor for a while and, eventually, the pain began to ebb away. Some of the other guys helped me up and, once I got back home, I didn't think any more about it, but that incident would come back to haunt me.

Loughborough was tough for athletes but, if you survived the system, you could do really well. They taught each athlete to be self-reliant. My training programme evolved to be more like a cyclist's than a runner's and so I felt even less a part of the athletics club. Now that I have developed as an athlete it can still be hard to fit into running sessions. I am slower than runners over the shorter distances but a lot quicker from around the 800 metres mark upwards. That means it can be challenging to find the right people to make the session worthwhile. I have trained at several different clubs but was happiest at Bridgend and, later on, at Cardiff AAC. They treated me as just another athlete. What I am not is a poor little cripple, a charity case or a little princess. It's the same with sponsorship. I have always wanted to be sponsored as an athlete or not at all. It has to be for the right reasons. When I first started in the sport it was quite hard to get financial support.

My first racing chair was bought for me in January 1987 by the Cardiff branch of the Rotary Club. It cost about £650 which seemed like a fortune to me. It was manufactured by a company called Bromakin and I used it in my first Paralympics in Seoul the following year. It made a huge difference having my own chair. At the time, it was the latest design with eight inch castors. It had no steering because the international rules didn't allow it then, but I thought it was really high tech. During the mid to late 80s there were a lot of advances made in terms of the technology of the chairs. The first three-wheelers came in around 1989. I remember Chris Hallam going to America and bringing one back and being very impressed. It's amazing how things have changed from when I had my Bromakin, but it was so nice not to have to borrow a chair from school.

Being at Loughborough helped me develop my strength. I look quite skinny but I can bench press one-and-a-half-times my own body weight. My power to weight ratio is good. If I hold my arms out horizontally my span is 5ft 10ins, which means I should have been really tall. Loughborough is a campus university and that was also a factor. Although I had the car, I'd push around as much as I could. The library was a mile-and-a-half away and I must have been doing about seven miles a day just from pushing about in my day chair. There was also a loop on campus which I could train on.

I started doing more local road races. Seoul and the Paralympics were a matter of months away but I was not focusing on that. I was just trying to get fit and be as fast as I could. I had no idea how the selection process for Seoul worked, so I didn't know how much of a chance I had of making the team. Each disability group had a certain number of places split among the different sports, but nobody knew how many places would be up for wheelchair athletes. So I kept training and hoping to be picked for international meetings. Seoul would be a bonus, but I knew I was borderline.

In April 1988 the National Disabled Student Games were held at Loughborough and I won the 60 metres and the 100 metres in times of 14 and 22 seconds. They were both records and I received my medals from Harry Carpenter, the television sports presenter. I was improving quickly through that year and was selected to represent Great Britain at an international event called the Nautilus International Wheelchair Classic in Dallas. That helped me get noticed. It also made me appreciate the level of Loughborough's reputation. I was picked up at the airport by a sports science student from the University of Texas at Arlington and when he found out I was from Loughborough, he couldn't stop apologising. 'I'm really sorry,' he said. 'The facilities here won't be anything like you're used to. It won't be a patch on Loughborough.' He was right when he said it would be different. We were competing at the football training ground at Arlington which had seating for thousands of people. Compared to Loughborough, with its sunken track surrounded by grass banking and locked gates, it was amazing. I told the student, 'You're right. This isn't like anything I'm used to.' I didn't tell him why, though, and he probably still thinks Loughborough has a 60,000 seater athletics stadium.

We were away for ten days and that was exciting, but the heat was incredible. It was a hot dry heat and temperatures were around 110 degrees, so all competition took place at night when it was a bit cooler. Most of the other athletes were Americans and Canadians, who were the people to beat at the time, so it was a true test. I was competing in the 100 metres, 200 metres and 400 metres. I didn't compete internationally over 800 metres at that point because I wasn't fast enough. I remember the jet-lag being a huge problem. I wasn't used to it and it hit me quite hard, but the races went well. I set personal bests in all three events and made a massive step forward. I came third in the 100 and 200 metres, but was fifth in the 400 metres after losing the plot coming out of the bend. There is no doubt that meeting helped my chances of getting on the plane to Seoul. Now it was just a question of wait and see.

Going to Dallas was significant in other ways, too, as I began to make some good friendships with other competitors. Among them were Chantal Peticlerc, a French-Canadian, and Daniela Jutzeler, a Swiss athlete. Daniela and I went on to become close friends. She could have a huge temper but was great fun to be around. She had more international experience than I did and helped me a lot in my first few years on the circuit.

I tended to do a lot of travelling on my own and most of my friends among my fellow competitors were from overseas. Rose Hill was my main rival in the UK but we never really got on. I think it was just down to the fact we were so different. Rose was in her early thirties and married with kids, while I was a student. The only thing we had in common was our racing. Rose's real strength was on the road, and that provided me with a massive incentive to do more road racing. Track racing was my first love and always will be, but road racing pays money. It also helped me grow stronger and faster for the track.

However, I was closer to Daniela than to most women in the British team and she was the nearest thing I had to an idol. I'd seen her race in the Nationals at Stoke Mandeville. She was one of the best in the world. She gave me her address and I stayed with her in Switzerland in 1989. As our friendship developed, we wrote to each other every six weeks or so.

Sometimes we'd talk about accidents we'd had. As a wheelchair athlete you have to presume every other road-user is coming out with the express intention of killing you. I have always been careful training on the roads because of how low we are. You have to think that nobody can see you. I wear bright clothes and a crash helmet. I started wearing a helmet while at Loughborough because a friend of one of my house-mates had been killed on the road, and many of the guys in the sport come into it because they have had traumatic accidents in cycling. My husband Ian is an example of this. He was a cyclist. Out training one day, he was sprinting with his head down and didn't even see the truck in front of him. He broke his back. Both of us have the attitude, 'Why worry about something you cannot change?' Ian got a first-class degree in chemistry and then a PhD – it didn't stop him doing what he wanted to do. However, for some people who go through such a trauma it can be very different. Other people we know who have had accidents have had to alter their lives completely and that can make it harder to deal with.

I have had a few crashes in my chair. I was hit by a car once. I was out training near my house in Birmingham when a woman pulled out of a garage without looking where she was going. Luckily, I wasn't going very quickly and saw what was going to happen, so I managed to push myself off the car. I escaped without a bruise but I was badly shaken up. Incidents like that make you think. It doesn't take much.

In the summer of 1988 my thoughts were concentrated on Seoul. It was by no means a certainty that I'd be in the team, but on the day I got home from university my mum gave me a pile of mail. There was a brown envelope with the wheelchair logo. I sensed what it must say because they didn't write to you if you weren't selected. I ripped it open. It was from the team manager. It took about half a second to realise what it said. I freaked out and shouted, 'I'm in! I'm in!' and handed the letter to Mum who started jumping around the kitchen. The part I remember most is the fact there was a tear-off slip at the bottom that you had to return if you wanted to go. It was as if it was a school trip or something. They still do that now, although the contracts they get you to sign get longer each time – things you are allowed and not allowed to do. Basically you have to promise to be a good girl while you are away and sell your soul to the British team!

It was an exciting summer knowing that I was going to the Paralympics. I actually went back to Loughborough because the roads on the campus were empty and better for training. I wasn't too confident about being on busy roads back then. I also knew I needed to do more miles and if I'd stayed in Cardiff, I would have ended up being distracted by my friends. So I went and stayed with one of the sub-wardens and his wife in their bungalow for a few weeks. I was sent no end of information and had lots of injections. Then the day of departure arrived. The team met up at Stoke Mandeville and we checked in our luggage. It was a long, boring flight, but there was still a sense of camaraderie and excitement. It wasn't long since I'd been watching Colin

Jackson and Linford Christie competing in the Olympics on television and now I was actually going there myself.

Some people like flying out at the last moment. I'm the opposite. I need to be in control of what I am doing and like to be settled in and know where everything is. On competition days I like to get to the venue hours ahead of time to make sure that I can plan for every eventuality. I don't trust many people and prefer doing things for myself. The first few days in Seoul were hard because it was my first time at a competition of this size and there was accommodation and accreditation to sort out. We were in a fourteen-storey tower block in the Paralympic village. There were two lifts in each building and ramps fitted to the ends of each building to make them accessible. The team was split into different disability groups rather than sports, so I was sharing a tiny apartment with two girls from the wheelchair basketball team. Being a wheelchair athlete usually means taking spare wheels and tyres, so there wasn't much room. I didn't bother unpacking and just kept everything under my bed in my kit bag.

Not long after we got settled in we heard an almighty racket. I looked out of the window and there were hundreds of people in banana yellow jogging bottoms and red satin jackets. We knew straightaway that it was the American team. It was the worst uniform that I have ever seen and not particularly conducive to keeping a low profile. Leading up to the Olympics there had been student riots against the American presence in Korea and they were warned not to go off site. The whole Korean culture was anti-America. I got a taste of how bad the situation was one day when I was walking near the edge of a village. Suddenly there was a lot of whistling and a group of guards descended on me. They just wanted to know what I was doing and then they were fine. They spent the next few minutes practising their English on me, but it showed the tensions that existed at that time. The Canadian team were told that they should always wear their team uniform outside the village and we tended to wear our GB kit as well. We always had police outriders travelling with us to the stadium.

We were in Seoul for quite a while before we competed, so we would go in to town for a couple of hours in the afternoon. There were lots of street markets with all sorts of weird things on offer and the first thing anyone would do is ask if we were American. When we said we were British we found that prices dropped immediately. I remember seeing a medicine man boiling hedgehogs in the street and there were lots of young girls with needle marks up and down their arms, standing on street corners, working as prostitutes. This was almost directly outside five-star hotels.

The Americans were oblivious to the hostility and couldn't see why there should be a problem. After we had finished competing, some friends, Dean Cavanagh, Andy Hodge, Pat Bailey and Paul Brennan, and I decided that we wanted to see some of the real Korea. So we went and visited the royal palaces and travelled to the border between the communist north and capitalist south. There were soldiers everywhere and we got a very strong impression of how vehemently the Americans were hated. We tagged on to the end of a tour around the war memorials built to honour the Americans who had died defending the line. It was an American tour and we were the only British there. Someone asked, 'How many Koreans died?' The guide barely broke breath and just said very matter-of-factly, 'Oh, a couple of million or something.'

I was nineteen and this was different from anything I'd experienced. When I'd known I was coming to Korea I'd gone to the library and read up on the country because, like everyone else, my only concept of the place was gleaned from MASH. It was exciting and interesting. Seoul was a culture shock for a teenager from Cardiff. I began to realise I'd lived a sheltered existence back home.

The Games lasted for just eight days. They had built a 60,000 seater stadium at a cost of £57 million. We joked among the team that it was like rent-a-crowd with the local churches coming along each day and picking different teams to support. The stadium was absolutely packed for the opening ceremony, though, and that was very spectacular. It allowed the people who couldn't afford to go to the Olympics to see what it had been like. Being British, we weren't allowed to be late, so we all got there about five hours beforehand with our packed lunches. The uniform was a grey skirt, white blouse with red and blue stripes in it, blue blazer and red bow tie. At the time I thought we looked quite smart, although I now know different. We had to wait around for hours. Eventually, we started moving and snaked under the stadium, following the other countries in alphabetical order. It was only at the last minute, when we turned and walked up over the ramp, that we could see the crowds and hear the noise inside. It was an incredible sight as we descended into the main body of the arena. The show included thousands of dancers, huge drums, karate displays, gymnastics and all sorts. In all my years competing, that is the most breath-taking opening ceremony I have been to.

There wasn't a great deal of expectation on me in Seoul, so I didn't feel much pressure. One more experienced athlete told me it takes a major competition to get used to the atmosphere and she was probably right. It is also the person who deals with the whole situation of being at a major competition like that who can win; it may not be the person who has been quickest all season. As usual, the athletes were weighing each other up on the warm-up track, which was next to the main stadium. That always happens. The men always try to show off and the women try to keep up with them as that's the best way of showing how quick you are. I don't like having many people around me when I am warming up and prefer not to talk to my rivals. If I can, I try to warm up with some of the guys. To set up the chair perfectly, you have to be going at your absolute top speed. That is not always easy when you are nervous prior to the race, but if some of the guys 'pull' me round I can draft, or slipstream, behind them which is an ideal way of achieving it.

I thought my best chance was in the 100 metres but I came fourth. I felt terrible. Pat Bailey had a very flashy video camera which he was taking everywhere. He'd started seeing a girl called Michelle so whenever he filmed any of us we would joke, 'Pat's missing Michelle.' It did the trick because they got together when he went home. Pat didn't video much after that 100 metre race, though, and I didn't feel like making jokes. My mood got worse when I blew the 200 metres completely. I just didn't get my head together and was annoyed because I'd been rushing to get there after doing the slalom. I hadn't wanted to do the slalom, but you had no choice in those days. The time scale was too tight and I didn't have time to prepare as well as I'd have liked. That left the 400 metres. I'd had a good semi-final, so was feeling pretty good, and came home third. I'd got a bronze. The time of 81 seconds was a new British record. It was a big moment and it was great to have some of my friends around me. You never get a huge amount of praise from other athletes because they are there with the same goals. If you're lucky someone might say, 'That was all right.' But you don't need people to pat you on the back and tell you what they think. You can tell from their faces and the way they react whether they are pleased or not.

I got back to the village and rang home as soon as I could. I had to queue for ages because everybody was doing the same thing. It was the middle of the night in Cardiff and I think Mum was more excited than I was. I just said, 'Hi, Mum, it's Tan. I've won a bronze.' She spent the next day ringing the local radio stations and newspapers. I was simply glad to be coming home.

There was quite a lot of recognition from people in my hall when I got back to campus. They had planned a secret party, put up loads of banners and baked a huge cake. Nikki tried to persuade me to go to the bar for a drink, but I was still jet-lagged and wasn't in the mood to go out. In the end she told me I had to go. My friends had also kept a diary of what had been going on while I was away. They had spent a lot of time doing it and I was quite touched. I'd missed a month of term, but it felt like a lot longer.

Mediawise, there was a lot less recognition as there hadn't been a huge amount of coverage of the Games. The powers that be weren't too bothered either. I'd only won a bronze and it was golds that mattered. But my headmaster from St Cyres, Mr Rowlands, nominated me for a *Sunday Times* award and I won the Student of the Year category. Andrew Neil, the editor of the paper, and Mary Peters, the Olympic legend, presented me with my prize, a £100 gift voucher, at a plush ceremony at Fishmongers' Hall in London. The event was sponsored by Moet et Chandon and so the champagne flowed very freely. It was fantastic to receive recognition in an open category rather than being pigeonholed in a category for disabled athletes. This was the way I wanted to be treated.

There were problems that needed facing, though. After missing a month's work, it was quite hard to slot back into the course. I'd been back two days when things went from bad to worse. I was sitting in an international relations lecture, struggling to understand what the lecturer was talking about, and swivelling around on my chair. Suddenly, I stopped and felt this incredible shooting pain running down my back. The lecture had about ten minutes to run so I stuck it out and went back to our house. I had tea with Nikki, who had moved in by that point, and went straight to bed. I could barely sleep and, by the morning, I couldn't even get out of bed. Nikki had to help me. She called the hall warden who took me to the medical centre where they told me I had a chest infection. I said, 'No I haven't, it's my back.' But they were oblivious. Then they said I might have a urinary tract infection, but I'd had quite a few of those as a child and knew it wouldn't feel like this. The people weren't helpful at all. They wouldn't transfer me to a local hospital and I was on the minimum dose of painkillers. I was too ill to argue. It was the worse pain I have ever felt.

Nikki rang my parents and they came straight up from Cardiff. I was being turned in bed when they arrived and they could hear screaming. Mum said, 'That's Tanni,' but Dad said it wasn't. He knew it was but was just trying to calm Mum down. The people at the med centre insisted there was no need for X-rays and were quite rude to my mum. They said it was a bladder problem because I was having hot and cold sweats but I could feel the metal rod moving at the base of my spine. You could actually see it coming through my skin. Mum put her foot down and announced she was taking me home to a hospital that would actually treat my condition. She had to sign a release form and they asked her if she knew how much she was putting me at risk by doing that. Mum had made up her mind and was not very polite to them. They asked how I was going to get home in the state I was in and Mum said, 'Well, you haven't been bothered about her so far.'

As I was leaving they asked what would happen if I was taken ill on the motorway. Mum has always been very matter of fact and just told them that she would stop and ring the emergency services. The problem was that by discharging myself it was taken that I was refusing treatment. That would make it hard to get admitted anywhere else. My parents have always made things happen, though, and they spoke to Dr Peter Gray, who I had seen as a child. He was the Professor of Paediatrics at the University Hospital in Wales and would know what to do. Sure enough, he got me admitted on a paediatrics ward and then transferred me. They knew straightaway that it was my back and, within hours, I had been X-rayed. The rod had come away at the bottom and the X-ray showed an infected area about two inches across. That explained the hot and cold sweats. The doctors were great. They put me on a massive dose of antibiotics and painkillers and started looking after me properly.

I wasn't scared at Loughborough but I was very frightened when I went down to the operating theatre in Cardiff. I can't stand the feeling just before being anaesthetised. There's that split moment where you feel yourself losing consciousness and you fight against it. You wonder whether you will come round. It's like being put down. I was crying and shouting that I didn't want the operation, but I didn't have any choice. That didn't make it any easier and I knew that, if they put a new rod in, I would have to be in a plaster jacket for another six months. After a long operation they managed to take the rod out and decided my spine looked stable enough without it. They had to leave the clips in, though, because the bone had knitted over them and there was no point trying to chip all that away.

In retrospect I think the rod came away when I fell from that rope when I was training with the mountaineering club. A couple of weeks after that I'd joined the scuba diving club. I had visions of it being really exotic, but the swimming pool at Loughborough was not exactly the Great Barrier Reef. The tank I had on my back was big and heavy and, after one session, I was in absolute agony. Now I realise why. The diving certainly didn't help. Throughout the year I had been forced to change my seating position in my racing chair because of the pain I was getting in my lower back. I didn't think anything about it, but my knees were getting higher and higher. The damage had already been done.

After the operation I was unrealistic about what I thought I could do. Mum and Dad wanted me to take it easy because it was major surgery. I was very weak. Mum says I asked her to push me once and that was when she knew how bad it was. The scar goes from the top of my neck down to the base of my spine. My parents were being quite protective of me at that point. I came out of hospital early because Sian, who was a nurse, was home and she could make sure the dressing was all right. But Mum was worried about me going back to Loughborough. It was one thing being at home with people running around after me, but another going back to lectures and student life. I don't think I really had much concept of just how big an operation it was.

We decided to do a trial run. Nikki was having a birthday party in the house at Loughborough so I went up for that to see how I coped. It was there that I realised I wasn't anything like as good as I thought. Nikki and some others noticed how long it was taking me to do things. I didn't bounce in and out of my chair like normal and was pale and tired. I finally went back to Loughborough in the sixth week of the second term. I'd done four days work in sixteen weeks, so I couldn't follow the lectures. I had stacks of course work to catch up on and had exams at the end of the year counting for forty-five per cent of my degree. I decided that it was too much to risk and thought that the only way was for me to drop out of my second year and start again. My department was supportive and I spoke to the local education authority because they had been paying my fees. I still stayed at Loughborough for the third term because I thought it would be better to be there if I was to get back into doing things for myself. I wanted to be independent, but it was hard.

After Seoul I'd been thinking about how much better I could do, but I lost a year of competition as well. Everything was put on the back burner and I spent that summer term just getting back to normal. At that time I was basically self-coached. Roy Anthony was back home in Bridgend and, with me being at Loughborough, it was difficult for him. So I spent most of my time in the sports science department at Loughborough when I should have been in the politics department. The great thing about Loughborough is that they have every training manual that anyone's ever written. I was a voracious reader and studied lots of them and devised my own programmes. Gradually, I started competing again and my times began to improve because I'd started doing more road racing.

When I went back to study again it was quite hard, having

missed a year. Although I didn't know anyone on the course – they were, effectively, the year below me – I actually found them more fun because they were not so politically-orientated. I also became very active with the Rag committee in our hall and we raised a lot of money for charity – Loughborough was one of the biggest university fund-raisers in the UK at the time. I thought it would be nice to do something useful at university and it was also a lot of fun.

Loughborough Rag had a double-decker bus. We would travel round the country in it with the aim of collecting as much money as possible. Part of the deal was we had to spend as little as possible, so we'd go to bakeries and supermarkets at closing time and ask for stuff they were about to throw out. They were so generous. In Bristol once we got invited to this restaurant and were fed pizza. It was a domino effect. One shop would give us something, word would spread and, before you knew it, we had as much as we could eat. Sometimes we didn't bother applying for the proper collecting licences on the understanding that we would call it a day if we were moved on by the police. One time in Worcester we had only been there for ten minutes when a representative from the charity we were collecting for saw us. She presumed that, as students, we were not to be trusted and called the police. I had to do some very fast talking to ensure nobody got arrested.

I graduated in 1991 with a 2.2 degree. By that time I knew wheelchair racing was what I wanted to do. I knew that I could make it if I worked really hard. Loughborough had been a struggle at times, but now I realise it was nothing personal. I felt bitter for a year but now I know that was the way they treated everybody. It wasn't a case of Loughborough being mean to me; it was just the general attitude to disability athletics in the late 1980s. I think it would be good to sit down with someone from Loughborough and talk about it because they still look at everything through rose-tinted spectacles. I don't think they realise how I feel about my time there. Now it is very different. Loughborough has become more co-operative because it has to be – athletes have more choice. When I was there a lot of people were very unhelpful.

Loughborough could be a tough place to be, but, in retrospect, it was probably the best training I could have received. Many of my friends from uni are still close and the chancellor, Sir Dennis Rourke, comes to the start line of the London Marathon every year to wish me well. He has followed my career from the time that I left university. That is the support that really matters. It gave me a lot of positive things and, above all, encouraged me to become the best athlete that I possibly could.

Chapter Four

Marathon Woman

WHEELCHAIR racing can be dangerous, fierce, bitter and frightening. It is not the tame second best some people might imagine. These factors add to the adrenaline rush you get as an athlete. As well as the threat from cars, the sheer speeds involved can be fraught with dangers. Sometimes we can reach 50 mph on the steep downhills. That is a real buzz. You know that one wrong move and it could end in disaster, and sometimes it does. There can be a fair number of crashes. The men are usually involved more than the women. That is because women tend to be more spread out and respectful of each other, while there are so many men that they sometimes cut each other up and come to blows.

There have been some notable crashes in men's racing. There was a huge one in the Boston Marathon one year, but the most spectacular was probably in 1992 at the Barcelona Paralympics in the 5000 metres. Helen Rollason, the BBC television presenter who became a good friend, filmed it. We went rushing over to her afterwards and asked for a copy of the tape. I said, 'That was the most amazing crash ever.' Helen wasn't sure whether she should run the film, but I said, 'If you show nothing else, show that.' I wanted her to do it because it showed what the sport was really like. The trouble is a lot of people don't want to see things like that because they don't like to see disabled people in trouble. It is a patronising view and it was important to show that crash because it proved we were not messing around. It showed us as athletes, not just a bunch of disabled people playing at sport. When Chris Boardman crashed in the Tour de France, that film clip was never off the television. He was on two wheels and we were on three. What was the big difference? I told Helen she had to run the film. She would have done if it was any other sport, so why not ours? Helen said, 'Right, let's do it then.'

So it was on the BBC and it got shown loads of times. It was brilliant. There is one point where Marc Quessey, a Canadian athlete, is upside down, flying through the air above the pack, before he crashes. Then the leader, Heinz Frei, who had got away from the pack, started to approach to lap them. He had his head down and was sprinting. All these officials were standing there not doing very much when they suddenly realised this man wasn't looking where he was going and hadn't seen the carnage in front of him. So they started picking up the mangled wreckage of frames and buckled wheels and throwing them off the track. Frantically, they started dragging athletes out of the way. I had my camera out because I thought he was going to plough straight into the back of these stricken athletes and their upturned chairs. The crowd held its breath. Heinz swerved, missed them, and carried on regardless.

I've had crashes of my own, so I know what it is like. Usually they have come in training rather than races, from hitting bumps in the middle of the road or not looking where I am going. One day I was out training with Sian, who used to follow me on her bike to keep me company. I heard a noise, turned round and there she was, lying on the pavement with her bike on top of her. A car had clipped her and she'd fallen off. In my sisterly way I couldn't help laughing out loud. A couple of weeks later, I was wiping my nose as I went through the hospital grounds near my parents' home in Cardiff. I was not looking where I was going, hit the kerb and went flying out. Sian got off her bike and came running up to me. To her credit, she didn't even snigger. I've done that a few times. At Loughborough in 1989 I crashed my new chair and flipped out. It was my first three-wheeler. It had a very short frame and so I wasn't very stable. Now I have one of the longest frames around made of light carbon fibre. It was a Wednesday afternoon, which was sports day, so everybody was out running. I was hugely embarrassed. Lots of people came over to see if I was all right, but I just said I was fine. I could taste blood. My mouth was caked in it, my left eye was shut and I was worried I'd broken my nose. But my pride was hurt more than anything. God, I look a mess, I thought. A guy who lived in the halls walked me back to make sure I was okay. I'd taken lumps out of my shoulder and sat in the bath, picking bits of gravel out of the wound. I had a black eye for ages, which caused a lot of jokes for weeks afterwards.

People might say my attitude to crashes is a bit callous and I think I do have a dark sense of humour. I am fairly cynical but not necessarily in a bad way. I'll only be rude to people I know, when I'm sure it won't come across wrongly. Ian and I have the same sort of mocking humour. For years people didn't even realise we were going out with each other because we weren't in the slightest bit romantic. When I told a friend I was getting married, she said, 'Really, who to?'

'Tommo, of course,' I replied.

She was staggered. 'You're joking. When did this happen?'

'Oh,' I said, 'about six years ago.'

They presumed we hated each other because that's how we were with each other. We share a caustic sense of humour that can be difficult to understand. Ian's worse than me. Even I don't understand his humour sometimes, so God help anyone else. He's very dry, bizarre and a bit surreal. He goes off at tangents and his favourite phrase is, 'Keep up.'

But the fact is cyclists are just as interested in crashes in their sport as we are in ours. It's an interesting and integral part of what we do. Being in a situation where you are close to losing it and somehow getting away with it is a thrill. When you go down a hill at 50 mph, you are living on the edge. A lot of the bad crashes occur in road racing because of the speeds involved. For instance, there is a 50 mph downhill in the Tyne Tunnel Race and there is a huge 40 mph slope near the start of the Boston Marathon. Because I don't weigh very much, I lose out on those fast hills. If someone weighs 15 kilos more than me, they can put 200 metres on me and that's a lot to catch up. But after Seoul I started doing more and more road racing and, as 1990 dawned, I knew I wanted to do one race above all others. Ever since I'd watched it on television as a girl in 1984, I'd wanted to take part in the London Marathon.

To be eligible for London I had to complete a full marathon beforehand. I chose the Porthcawl Marathon, which was an open event for men and women, at the end of 1989. By that point I was back training fairly normally after having the rod out of my back. The marathon was a goal for me and definitely helped my recovery. On the day of the race it poured down. I had spiky hair and the gel kept running into my eyes and stinging. The course comprised eight laps of a three-mile loop around the town. It was freezing and I wasn't totally prepared for that sort of distance. I hadn't done anything like the mileage I should have. My time was a pretty pathetic 3 hours 3 minutes, but I hadn't expected to do anything and was just happy to have finished. It was a huge amount of fun and I was ready for London.

Before that there was the small matter of the Commonwealth Games in Auckland. There was to be an 800 metres demonstration race for women and a 1500 metres for men.

People often ask me what's the difference between demonstration and exhibition races. Basically, demo races are a step down – you have no rights and it means you have no chance of gaining full medal status. At the Olympics it means you're excluded from the Olympic family. Demo races were first held at the Olympics in 1984. The Paralympics were supposed to go to the States, but they decided they couldn't put them on so they selected a couple of events. They chose two wheelchair races because America was good at them at the time, and also they'd be over fairly quickly. People like the fact that athletes in wheelchairs don't look too disabled. They are comfortable with that.

At first the New Zealand Paralympic and Physically Disabled Federation did not invite Wales to submit any entries, but Chris Hallam and I managed to get in at the last minute. I was really keen to go as I've always been proud of my Welsh roots. People always assume I'm English but I'm not. I'm Welsh and proud of it. England and Scotland didn't get the forms through in time to send athletes, so Chris and I flew out on our own to represent Wales. We soon realised there would be problems. The Welsh Commonwealth Games Association refused to give either of us any kit because their view was we were Mickey Mouse athletes. We had no recognition, but eventually they gave us one vest between the pair of us. I'd known Chris since 1987 and, initially, we didn't get along. He is very self-assured but that trip made a big difference to our relationship. Once I got to know him I realised it was all front and that, beneath the surface, he is a big softie. We ended up staying with the other athletes who were in the exhibition races. It was a million miles away from the plush quarters where the non-disabled athletes were staying and I ended up doing the washing up next to one of the women I was going to be competing against. It was an odd arrangement and, right up until the last minute, we didn't even know if the event was going to go ahead. There was a lot of uncertainty about what was happening.

Finally, it did take place on the same day as the men's 800 metres and I remember watching Seb Coe race. I came third in a time of 2 minutes 27 seconds, beating my personal best. Then I gave the vest to Chris. I didn't have time to wash it. It was baggy on me and tight on him, so Chris kept going on about how my chest wasn't big enough. That was typical Chris. He came fourth. We weren't allowed medals or a presentation at the track, so we got the bus back to our base and had a little ceremony among ourselves. The New Zealand Paraplegic Association had got little medals made.

There was no contact with the non-disabled athletes and none of them showed any interest in us. We were completely excluded. At the time I was prepared to accept all that because it was the only way things could happen. Some of the Canadians were more outspoken because they were used to having good integration. I wasn't close enough to anyone from Welsh Athletics or the Commonwealth Games Committee to know why it had to be like this. I didn't know enough about the system, but that began to change between Seoul and Barcelona. After the Commonwealth Games I wanted to find out more. Your level of influence is dependent on your knowledge and so I set about finding out why we were treated like this. Having to share a vest with Chris was archaic. It was like something from the Dark Ages.

Back home from Auckland I stepped up my training for the 1990 London Marathon. I was doing about forty miles a week, but that was still nowhere near the eighty to a hundred I do now. I was excited by the prospect of competing in the London race. It's a major event because of the publicity it attracts. It is the only time that you see élite wheelchair racers battling it out on mainstream television. We all stayed in the same hotel the night before, but I didn't sleep very well and got up feeling like death warmed up. That has since become my routine. I generally feel progressively worse on the day of a big race until I am physically sick. I've become quite famous for it. It's almost a trademark. I can't keep anything down beforehand and now I just have a liquid meal, so at least there's something in my stomach. I've seen dietitians and spoken to a psychologist, but it's just nerves. There's nothing I can do about it. Ironically, it's worse during marathons when there is not so much to lose – track racing is more important to me. Up until about 1997 I was fine racing on the track and wouldn't throw up at all, but even that's got worse as I've got older. I was sick before three of my four finals in Sydney.

I think it happens because when I get a runny nose, I feel sick, and when I'm nervous, my nose runs. It's a knock-on effect. For someone so small I produce buckets of the stuff. Before the demonstration race at the Sydney Olympics, my friend Dan Saddler was saying how brilliant it was because I hadn't been sick. I went away and did a warm-up lap and then I felt it coming. I said to Dan, 'Just sit there and block me from the cameras.'

And I threw up right by the Canadian tent. Usually I know when it's coming, so I can control it and make sure it is on my own terms. However, sometimes that doesn't work. I threw up right in front of the BBC cameras on the start line of the Dublin Marathon one year, but the worst was probably in the Batley 10k. There were eighteen of us on the start line and I just said, 'Oh, oh, I'm going to puke.' I pushed my way up the road to find a drain and an official approached me, tapping his watch. 'You've got to be on the grid and if you're not then you can't race,' he said. I looked at him and heaved. He stepped back and said, 'Take as much time as you want.'

At London there is special transport laid on to take you to the start. I sat on the bus with my rivals and that was quite strange. I didn't like it because of the control aspect. I'd rather have been there much earlier, so I could have had more time to prepare. There was no real practical need because I'd checked everything a million times the night before. It's just the way I am. The bus from the hotel took forty-five minutes. I started to see people in their tracksuits walking to the start and the adrenaline began to pump through my veins. Then we got to Blackheath and there were thousands of people there. The wheelchair racers had their own enclosure near the start for their warm-up. It was only about 200 metres long, but I pushed up and down there to get warm. It was cold at the start and the rain was sheeting down. I saw John Harris, an athlete I knew from Wales, and spoke to him. There was a joke going round about how I couldn't push very far because I was so little, but I didn't care. I was just happy to be there. I was nervous but not worried. When you are in a chair you know you're going to get through the race; it's just a question of how long it takes.

There were around sixty chairs on the start line – in those

days men and women started together – so it was the biggest field I'd been in. I was on the second row, next to Rose Hill. Her personal best was around 2 hours 50 minutes. My training had gone a lot better since Porthcawl, so I knew I could break 3 hours. By the 4 mile stage the field started to string out. Connie Hansen and Ingrid Lauridsen, two Danish athletes, disappeared. Connie went with the men's pack for a while but began to struggle a bit in the rain. She carried some glue with her, used that to get a better grip and got back to the front of the pack. She ended up beating a lot of men which didn't do their egos any good. I remember being caught by runners at about the 12 mile point. That can be difficult because runners and chairs take different lines. Sometimes you have to cut through the runners to get to the other side of the road. It's a problem because you don't want to take any of them out, but you don't want to lose too much time. They have as much right to be there as we do, but sometimes there are crashes and chairs have taken runners out. Touch wood, it's never happened to me.

I got away from Rose at the start. I was trying to push hard all the way. John Harris and another athlete, Chas Saddler, had both stopped to fix punctures. I caught them up and we carried on together until I got a puncture at 21 miles. When it's raining, the water washes a lot of grit and debris on to the road, so there are more punctures than normal. John and Chas stopped and helped me fix it. John was really quick and it only took a few minutes but, while we were stopped, Rose went past. That was an awful feeling. To make matters worse, I hit the wall. I picked up a high-energy drink from one of the stations around the course, but it was way too strong for me and I began to feel woozy. All I was thinking about was catching Rose. I went flat out to catch her. If I could get close, I knew I'd have a chance. Rose's strength was maintaining a good speed throughout, but I had a better sprint finish. Then a mile from the end I started to get blurred vision. I couldn't see very well at all. I knew I was losing it and my arms were dead. I ended up fourth in 2 hours 49 minutes and Rose was third. By way of a variation I threw up on the finish line. That was the point at which my rivalry with Rose really started. It's not nice being beaten by anybody, but at least Connie was the world number one and Ingrid was up there with her at the time. Rose and I were both developing quickly. She was a powerful motivator for me.

When I crossed the line I was wrapped in tinfoil and given a bag containing my medal, some sandwiches and a Mars bar. Everything hurt. My hands were covered in blisters. My muscles were numb and I was incredibly tired. Despite losing to Rose, I'd broken 3 hours and taken 15 minutes off my personal best, so I was quite happy. At first you think, why do I do marathons? But then you forget the pain and soreness and there is a nice feeling that comes from knowing you have done everything you could. It's masochism. I enjoy pushing myself to the limits and I love that feeling you get when you don't know whether you are going to pass out or puke.

There is a collection point near the finish and some changing facilities. I am always aware of how awful I must smell at the end of a marathon. You feel horrible. Then it's back on the bus and back to the hotel. I didn't hang around and drove home to Cardiff that afternoon. By the time I'd reached my parents' house, I'd stiffened up so much that I couldn't move. I had to toot the horn and Mum and Dad came out. I couldn't even open the door so they had to lift me out of the car. Mum thought that was highly amusing.

When I look back on my first London Marathon, the most significant thing was John and Chas stopping to help me. That is not a normal occurrence in wheelchair racing. People usually just leave you, but they had both decided that their times were not going to be anything special because of their own punctures. It was still a pretty amazing gesture. Nobody had stopped for me since and I've never stopped for anyone else. Once I was in the Torfaen Half Marathon with Ian and his chair broke. I was some distance behind him but could see him sitting at the top of a hill. I thought, why's he stopped? As I got closer, I realised it wasn't a puncture and that his frame had snapped in half. It had happened at the top of a huge hill. If it had been thirty seconds later he would have been travelling at around 45 mph and would have been wiped out. I thought, thank God it's happened there and not the other side.

I looked across at him and said, 'Are you okay?'

'Yes,' he replied. So I put my head back down and carried on.

Afterwards, he pretended that he wasn't best pleased. 'Why didn't you stop?' he asked.

I said, 'You were fine. You weren't lying on the side of the road. There wasn't any blood. There was someone there to take you to the finish line.' He didn't really expect me to stop. It was nothing to worry about. Stopping wouldn't have helped.

The only other time I've punctured in a race was in the 2000 London Marathon. On that occasion I was on my own and it took a lot longer to fix. I had an expensive pair of tyres, costing around £130, and they were very tight. Even though there was not a great amount of glue, I struggled to get the tyre off. Then, once it was fixed, I couldn't get enough air back in. I'd checked it the night before and it had gone up fine, but I just had a hand pump in the marathon and there was a problem with the valve. I ended up pushing very slowly, averaging only 13 mph. It was a miserable marathon.

There is no question that it is not as taxing to do a marathon in a wheelchair as it is to do one on foot. We are not hauling our body weight around and can take a breather. We do not hurt as much and if you put the training in, you are usually fine. But there are no short cuts in wheelchair racing. You need to put in hours in a chair. There's a lot of skill involved, as well as stamina and strength. When I started out I wasn't doing the right amount of training. If a race is twenty-six miles long and you are pushing thirty miles a week in training, it is going to be hard. I always find the 16 to 19 miles stage the hardest bit in my marathon. You get to the 16 mile point and you know there are another ten miles to go. That can be psychologically draining. It's also hard when you get to 13. That is halfway and if you are feeling bad at that point, you know there is no hope. At London they make it worse by having balloons and banners at the halfway stage. You get that 'Oh, my God' feeling. It always seems to take an eternity from 13 to 18, but if you can get to 20, you'll be fine. You have six left and that's not a problem. If you have a good marathon, it's the most amazing feeling. I love being in a pack. It suits the way I push. I hate time trialling because I hate being out on my own. In a pack there is always something happening. There is no better sensation than being in a group, coming up for a sprint finish after twenty-six miles.

At first I didn't think I would be able to make a career out of wheelchair racing. Some of the American guys and the top Europeans were managing to do it, but I wasn't doing enough road racing. I was being coached through an athletics club at

Loughborough where the feeling was you couldn't be a sprinter and do marathons. It is different for wheelchair racers, though, and almost everyone competes at all distances. Between Seoul and Barcelona I came into contact with a lot more athletes and began to realise that being good on the road would benefit my track events and vice-versa. We are lucky as wheelchair athletes because, unlike non-disabled runners, we can compete in everything from the 100 metres to the marathon. That's because we don't use weight-bearing muscles – we're overcoming momentum not gravity. You have to put in the miles on the road even if you are a sprinter, so everyone competes in a wide range of events.

Throughout 1990 my performances began to pick up. I went to the World Championships in Assen, Holland, and came second in the 100 metres and 200 metres. A week later I beat Ingrid Lauridsen in the marathon at the World Wheelchair Games at Stoke Mandeville. My time of 2 hours 20 minutes was almost half an hour faster than I'd managed at London. When I returned to Stoke Mandeville for the same meeting a year later, I made a breakthrough, but it was tainted by controversy. I won the 100 metres and the 200 metres and, just as significantly, beat Ingrid in those events for the first time. My elation at managing that was tempered when a storm blew up over my technique in the marathon.

Chris Hallam was in charge of the team and he decided that we should do all we could to ensure that either Rose or myself won it. The race was being used for selection for another race in Japan. Ian had already been selected, so he didn't need to compete, but we made a deal that he would and that he would help either Rose or myself around the course. He would work with whoever reached him first. That was me. I was better at hills than Rose and there was a steep one near the start. I stuck with Ian and won, but some other racers complained about the tactics we had used. They said it was unfair to draft behind someone else, as that provides shelter and enables you to go quicker. In effect, you are in a faster racer's slipstream. At the time, the rules were not very clear on it. I felt a bit guilty afterwards that I'd beaten Ingrid in that way. It wasn't cheating but I suppose it was bending the rules. Sometimes it is considered acceptable and sometimes it is not. People try to do it all the time, but I wasn't doing it for long in the race. Now, in the big races, they have separate starts for men and women, so you can't do it, but that's not down to me.

I think Chris had expected Rose to be the one to reach Ian first. But when I reached Ian, Rose was about 100 metres back and we couldn't wait around for her because gaps open up too quickly. That incident added to the competitiveness between us. Rose came second in the 1991 London Marathon and I was way back in third. The rivalry between us was growing.

Although it is the race I have become synonymous with, the fact is the London Marathon is not a particularly strong event for women wheelchair racers. The problem is it clashes with the Boston Marathon and a lot of the élite athletes go there instead. The prize money in Boston is $20,000 whereas the best it has ever been in London is £800. For years we weren't allowed any prize money at all, while they tempt the top non-disabled runners with £30,000. That's a shame because it means London doesn't attract the best athletes. The biggest women wheelchair field to have entered is ten. It's a problem that needs addressing.

We have lots of juniors competing in wheelchair racing, but find it difficult to attract them to marathons. That is partly because it is such a big commitment. You have to put in an awful lot of hours and it can be a lonely exhausting experience. Not many women are prepared to put themselves through that. Tennis and basketball are taking all the women in wheelchair sport because they are a lot more fun than flogging your guts out for fifteen miles a night. I can understand that. Had basketball been more developed when I was growing up, I'd have done that instead, but there weren't any teams in the area. We need to re-evaluate the junior programme. You need under-seventeen, nineteen and twenty-one age groups, as they do in mainstream athletics. Now, you get to eighteen and you are lumped in with the seniors. You go from doing cosy events, like schools and regionals, to nationals where you are racing me and Dave Holding. It's not a lot of fun if you are competing in an 800 metres and getting beaten by 300 metres. We should monitor our kids better and provide a stepping stone for them to graduate to seniors. We also need to make the racing chairs cheaper. If they cost £1,200 that is outside most parents' budgets and it's pretty miserable doing a marathon in a day chair. There's huge mark-up on race chairs so there is scope for bringing the prices down.

By 1992 the media interest in wheelchair athletics was gathering pace. Chris Hallam was even used on some of the posters to advertise that year's London Marathon and there were a few bits on television. For me, winning in London was not the important thing. With a lot of the top racers in Boston, my main priority was setting a fast time. Rose and I stayed together for the entire race that year. We spent twenty-six miles working really hard to get rid of each other, but didn't exchange a single word the whole way. She tried to get away from me on the Embankment because she realised that if it came to a straight sprint, I'd have a better chance. For the last mile I was really hanging on because she was upping the pace and trying to open up a lead. It came down to a sprint finish and I finally managed to edge ahead with about 200 metres to go. I eventually won by two chair lengths. It was a great race and a fast time too (2 hours 22 minutes), so there was a real buzz at the end. It was a perfect way to start Paralympic year – a season I'd been concentrating on for so long.

One of the great things about being an athlete is getting to compete in different parts of the world. I have done marathons in America, Germany, Spain and Switzerland as well as the UK. One of my best came in 1993 in Heidelberg. It was a beautiful course that stretched up and down the river. I might have won it too had Daniela not pushed me into a pile of cones near the end! She did it because she didn't want me to get past Connie Hansen. I don't push people, but a lot of the women do and Ian says I should join them. It is an example of how nasty the racing can get. Daniela was a great friend but she had no qualms about pushing me off the road. What made it stranger was the fact that Daniela, Connie and I were all sponsored by Top End. But Daniela used to domestique for Connie, which meant she would try to block people off. That still happens. A lot of athletes work together like that, a bit like bike teams in the Tour de France but less formalised. I've been asked to do it myself and it has been suggested by sponsors that it might be useful, but I just say, 'I'll see what I can do,' and ignore them. I'm too bothered about trying to win to worry about helping anyone else.

Daniela and Connie were working really hard against Lily Angrenny. They dropped me at about 19 miles and it took me 1.5 miles to reel them back in. It was going to come down to a sprint finish between the four of us. Nobody was concerned about Lily's sprinting, but Connie and Daniela had good kicks and so did I. Daniela was blocking for Connie as we neared the straight. I tried to come through and that's when Daniela reached out and shoved me into some traffic cones. I lost a lot of ground and by the time I'd recovered, they had got clear. I tried to pick it up and might have won if there had been another 100 metres, but there wasn't enough time. Connie won and went off to the victory ceremony. It's just part of racing and I didn't blame her or Daniela. I blamed myself for not coming through faster.

Lily is an athlete I like very much, but I feel she gets a rough deal sometimes. She is fair and works very hard. She will always give 110 per cent, but some racers take advantage of that and let her do all the donkey work. They are quite mean to her. To make matters worse for her, she is one of only a few racers not sponsored by Top End. That means the Top End women often gang up on her. It's not fair. Even when I was with Top End, I'd work with Lily because I knew she would never try to stitch me up. Some of the other women would do deals with each other and try to cut you up near the finishing line, but not Lily.

I was talking to Lily on the start line of the Berlin Marathon in 1993. It was one of my best races. We decided we'd try to pick people off as the race went on, but after about 200 metres, she turned to me and said, 'Tanni, we're going.' I wasn't about to argue. We got to the front and helped each other out. First I'd kick and then she would. We took it in turns. It went well until about halfway and then I started struggling to keep on the pace. We had been doing a minute at the front each, but Lily knew I was in trouble, so she started doing two minutes to every one of mine. That was the way she was. She helped people out. Finally, at 18 miles she dropped me. I was just so knackered, but I managed to fight my way back and joined the back of a men's pack. They decided they didn't want to be seen pushing with a woman, so they picked up the pace again, but I stuck with them. I came through and finished second. Lily won the race. If it wasn't going to be me I was glad it was her. She is just a really nice person to work with.

Berlin is one of the most interesting marathons that I have done. I did it when the Wall had just come down and it was the first time the race had gone into both sides of Germany. You could tell the difference immediately. In the west the roads were all nice and smooth, the apartment blocks were colourful and there were posters all over the place. By contrast, the east was dark and depressing with broken-down Trabants littering the roads. What didn't change from east to west was the noise. It was deafening. People were furiously banging saucepans and cowbells for the entire course. I remember thinking I can't stand this for much longer. It was as if someone was banging you over the head for twenty-six miles. We went through the Branden-burg Gate and there were bits of the Wall lying all around. It was an interesting experience. After the race, I went and looked round the Reichstag. You could sense the history.

A year after coming second to Lily in Berlin, I won London for the second time. It was another long battle with Rose. I hadn't raced well in 1993 and had come third, and that made me more determined the following year. We had a different start from the men and, to be honest, it looked stupid as there was only a handful of us there. I couldn't see the point, but Rose was all for it because she knew that I had a better start and could get going with the men's pack if we started together. I was stronger at the beginning and she was better in the middle and towards the end. It came down to sprint finish again and I just beat her to the line. That was the way it was for quite a few years – Rose and I battling it out around the UK. It was great to win London, but the way I judge myself is by comparing how I race against men. I knew the top people were in Boston and, after winning London for a second time, I decided I would go there myself the following year.

I still went to London in 1995 as a spectator and stayed at a hotel with a bunch of other racers. I was looking forward to going to Boston, even though I knew the course was not well suited to me because of all the downhills. The morning of the London Marathon, I had breakfast with a lot of other athletes and they couldn't believe it as I stuffed my face with Danish pastries while they tucked into their muesli and bananas. My inability to keep food down had become a standing joke, so they were surprised to see me gorging myself like that.

It was always freezing in London but, of course, this year it was warm. Everyone was wandering around in T-shirts. And then I flew out to Boston where there were subzero temperatures and I had to go and buy lots of extra training kit because it was so cold. Sian came with me and sat in the car with the heater turned on full while I went out training. I saw her tapping the side of her head as if to say how stupid I was. She had a point. There was a violent wind and I remember pushing flat out into it and reaching about 3 mph and then turning round and absolutely flying back. I began to think how daft I'd been to forsake London for this.

Louise Sauvage, a friend and fellow racer, flew out and stayed with us before the race. We found a little village just north of Boston, with a café, a post office and a bar. It was very quaint and the people were friendly. We had a great time. The race itself was not so good. I'd got a new chair and hadn't fixed the wheel on properly. It started to come loose, so I had to stop and fix it. Then there was Heartbreak Hill. That comes at 17 miles and lasts for 2.5 miles. It seemed like an eternity. You'd think you were nearly at the top, but then you would turn a corner and be faced with another climb. To make it worse, all these Americans had decided that was the best place to have their barbecues, so the smell of frying onions and hot-dogs drifted along the air. I adore that smell and thought, I could just stop and fight you for that hot-dog. It was torture. That's the hardest bit of any marathon I've been in. Boston's also a very bumpy course and the finishing straight is never-ending. I finished sixth and felt horrible. I was cold and starving hungry. I met Lou who had come second and we went to find Sian, who had the keys to the car. We'd agreed to meet under the letter G at the meeting point, but we couldn't find her. So we both started screaming, 'Sian, Sian, Sian!' People looked at us as though we were mad, but we were desperate to get inside.

I enjoy marathons. They test your resolve and determination. They push you to the limits of endurance. London will always be close to my heart and it's amazing how it's developed over the years. When I first went there, you would find big gaps in the crowd, but now the only places where there aren't people watching are in the underpasses. People know my name now. Everywhere I go I hear people shouting, 'Come on, Tanni,' which is lovely. Some people don't share that view, though. A few years ago I was pushing with another Welsh athlete, Rich Powell. After six or seven miles, he said, 'I'm pissed off pushing with you.'

I was a bit shocked because he is a good mate. 'Why?'

'Because all I get is "Tanni this, Tanni that" all the bloody time. It's driving me mad.'

A lot of road races attract just a smattering of spectators, so it can be like training. London's different. I added three more wins in 1996, 1998 and 2001, but I don't view any of my five victories there as being among my best marathons. Ironically, the races I consider my best were ones I didn't win – Heidelberg in 1993 when Daniela pushed me off the track, and Lake Sempach in Switzerland in 2000. I hadn't done enough mileage in the run-up to that one and died in the last two miles, but I still clocked 1 hour 48 minutes, which was a minute inside my personal best. I think I can go quicker. My aim is to do 1 hour 41 in a marathon and I believe I can do that at Sempach because it's a flat, fast course with smooth roads and good weather conditions.

For the 2001 London Marathon I agreed to having a camera on my chair and being miked up for the BBC. Initially, I was a bit worried about that because the language can sometimes get a bit choice in the middle of a pack. It was funny, though, because everybody was on their best behaviour and acting very out of character. It was all, 'Would you mind awfully moving out of the way?' and 'How are you feeling?' I thought, what are you talking like that for? That's not normal. It wasn't a strong field, so I agreed to the camera, even though it weighed 2 kilos. I thought it was important because it gave a new perspective on wheelchair racing.

There are still a lot of people who don't like us being in the London race. There have been lots of letters in *Athletics Weekly* saying how boring the racing is, how we are not real athletes and what a disgrace it is that we are shown on television. One bloke wrote in and said he had even seen a 'so-called disabled athlete' get out of his chair, as if all wheelchair racers have to be paralysed. It shows the ignorance we come up against. In the early years the organisers didn't want a wheelchair marathon, but Ken Livingstone said there wouldn't be a marathon unless wheelchair racers were involved. It's only in recent years that there has been more co-operation, but London needs to figure out what it wants to do with the wheelchair marathon. At the moment, only élite racers are eligible, which is why the field is so small, especially with many of them choosing to go to Boston instead.

Where London has been crucial is in raising the profile of the sport. It's not the best race because of the small field, bumpy course and the amount of downhills which mean the athletes get spread out, but it is the one that keeps the sport in the public consciousness. It also keeps Nike, my sponsors, happy for a year if I do okay at London. It is a positive event because it gets wheelchair athletics on television and links it to an event that has a lot of credibility. Personally, it has been important. My first win there in 1992 was a breakthrough for me. And, though I didn't know it then, it was the beginning of a golden year.

Chapter Five

Reigning in Spain

DATELINE 4 September 1992. This is it. For the last four years I've been thinking about the Paralympics. Now, after all the waiting and training, I'm on the start line for my first race, the heats of the 400 metres. Ingrid Lauridsen is on my outside. I know she is the main threat. If I can beat her I will be in with a great chance. I have been through my usual warm-up. I get in my chair an hour before the race and then, twenty minutes beforehand, I start doing regular laps. I try to stay relaxed. I'm in the chair longer than most athletes, but I'm probably more paranoid than most. I always add extra time to make sure I'm not rushed. I guess I'm obsessive. With an hour to go, I'm not at my most rational so I don't want someone coming over to me and talking about my summer holidays. I'd rather be alone.

I've thought about the race a million times running up to the Games, so I don't want to go over it all again. The closer it gets to the start of the race, the more I look at my watch. The nerves begin. We get six minutes on the track before the start. I spend the time looking for my family. They are not hard to spot because, as usual, they have two flags with them, a Union Jack and the Welsh dragon. I always like to know where they are before I race. It's another aspect of the routine and it also helps

Warming up for the 400m final in Barcelona, 1992.

Winning the 100m in Barcelona, with Ingrid Lauridsen in second place.

Looking to the scoreboard to see my time after winning the 100m in Barcelona, 1992.

Barcelona 800m. Ann Cody celebrates . . . before being disqualified.

Barcelona 800m. An unexpected Gold.

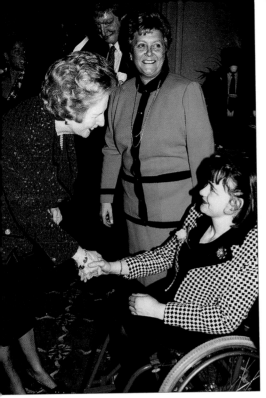

Meeting the Prime Minister at the People's Award, 1992.

Daniela, who tragically died in 1994; she is still missed in our sport.

1992 – promoting Children in Need.

Australia's Louise Sauvage competing in the World Championships, Stuttgart, 1993.

Berlin Marathon, 1993 – I came second. Lily Anggreny won and Daniela was third.

Louise Sauvage teasing me about my pre-race routine!

Meeting Welsh royalty!

Travelling the States with Jenni Banks, my coach.

My second London Marathon win.

Hard in training before the 1994 World Championships.

My husband Ian representing England in the Commonwealth Games. Ian is my greatest supporter . . . and critic!

Berlin, 1994 with some local supporters.

Wearing number 6 in the 1994 European Championships. We all wore black armbands in memory of Daniela. Her funeral was on the same day as the race.

kill time. If I'm busy looking for them it stops me thinking about what I've got to do.

Finally the waiting is over. We line up. My plan is to go out as hard as I can and just have a good one. Along with the 200 metres, this is my best event. I am confident and I know it's going well early on because I'm catching Ingrid. Technically, it is one of my best ever 400 metres. I get each sector spot on. I go flat out for the first 100, steady for the next 100 and then kick at 200 and 300. I cross the line first and immediately look up at the board to see the re-run of the last 10 metres. Then I see the time – 59.20. *WORLD RECORD* flashes up on the screen in huge letters. It takes a while to sink in. At first I think the clock must be wrong. Every time I've looked up before it's always said one minute something. Then I realise I'm the first woman to go under a minute. I do a lap of honour and get off the track and go to meet Sian, Dad and my boyfriend, Andy. I've got a huge grin on my face. There are a lot of other guys from the team there. One of them says, 'Your start looked a bit slow.' Another says, 'Yeah, and your pick-up wasn't great.' I think, here we go. Then someone says, 'That wasn't bad,' which is something. Dad's quite calm but glowing with a huge smile and Sian is jumping around like a nutcase. It's so exciting and I am on such a high. It's the start of an incredible summer.

I'd vaguely started looking for jobs when I finished university in 1991 but Sian suggested I had a year off to concentrate on Barcelona. Dad gave me a cheque for £2,000 for that year which was really nice and helpful and then my grandmother gave me money to go to Australia for three weeks. That trip was a break-through for me. I train well in warm weather and I was in good form. I broke the 200 metres world record at the Victoria State

Games and just missed out on the 400 and 800 metre records. I knew I was pushing well and during that trip I made a huge amount of progress.

The build-up to Barcelona began in earnest with the trials for the Olympic 800 metre demonstration race. Under the rules, we were allowed to have the final at the Olympics. The trials were held in whichever country wanted to host them. New Orleans was hosting the US track and field trials, so they offered to take the wheelchair trials too. In all my career I have never competed anywhere so hot and humid. When I got there I went training, but couldn't push more than 200 metres. I tried doing a few sprints and remember thinking, this is horrific. I'm never going to be able to complete 800 metres, let alone qualify. I couldn't breathe. The track was blue and I wasn't used to that either. It doesn't make a huge amount of difference, but there are only two in England and it was quite hard on the eyes.

Luckily, they held the race late in the day when it was not so humid and that helped a lot. I came third in my heat and that was good enough for me to qualify for the Olympics. It was a big thrill. I knew that I'd be going to Barcelona in a month's time and it was exciting to think I'd made it through in an event dominated by T4 athletes. I should explain the different categories in wheelchair racing. Basically, it is split into four. T1 is for tetraplegics with very severe impairments of the arms. T2 is also for tetras but they are ones who are paralysed from the chest down. T3 is my class and is for those paralysed from roughly the waist down. It means you have got no stomach or lower back muscles and no hip flexes. That makes a massive difference when racing because you don't have the stability to hold your body down at the start. What happens is my body moves upwards, so I don't get a fast start. The T4 athletes can be people who are leg amputees or have broken their backs. They can be stable in the chair and get off much faster. T3s and T4s are usually kept separate for the 100, 200, 400 and 800 metres, but go together from the 1500 metres upwards. For the trials we were all lumped together, so for me to make it in an 800 metre race meant I had to have the most amazing start of my life.

I had some trouble getting kit to compete in, which brought me back down to earth. Eventually, the treasurer of British Athletics had a word with the British Olympic Association (BOA) and I got a British tracksuit. They wouldn't let me have the full kit, but it was something. Because we were a demonstration event, we weren't allowed to stay in the village, so we were stuck out in a hotel. I was sharing with Jean Driscoll, one of the top American athletes and a rival. That was strange. I'd also been told by the International Olympic Committee (IOC) liaison officer that we weren't allowed to take our coaches, but when I got there I found everybody else had theirs. In the end I had the French men's coach looking after me because he'd been to demo events before. It was a bit surreal. One minute I was thinking, God, I'm at the Olympics and the next I'm thinking, God, it should be more organised than this.

We didn't have any contact with the non-disabled athletes, but I went to watch Colin Jackson race because he is Welsh and I vaguely knew him from Cardiff. There'd been a lot of hype surrounding his race and everyone thought he was going to get the gold, so I wanted to be there. That ended up being a saga in itself. I couldn't get any transport, so I walked two miles to the main bus route. When one turned up I jumped out of my chair and dragged it on after me, but a Spanish official wasn't having any of it. He started shouting, 'No, no, no,' grabbed me by my T-shirt and pulled me off. I only knew about ten words of Spanish, so I didn't have much choice. I tried to creep back on when he wasn't looking, but he caught me and kept pointing to the floor. A couple of minutes later another bus with a lift came along. He'd been trying to tell me that I didn't need to clamber on to the bus because an accessible one was coming along. I got on and this very sweet Spanish man, with whom I'd been grappling minutes earlier, smiled and waved.

It took four-and-a-half hours to get to the stadium because of the traffic, but I got the perfect seat right by the finishing line. There were loads of British supporters there rooting for Colin and the atmosphere was fantastic. It all seemed worth it. Then the gun went off and everybody stood up. I couldn't see a thing. I couldn't even glimpse the board with the screen on. It was quite funny really. I spent half a day getting to the track to watch Colin and still missed it. It took a few minutes before I even knew he'd lost and it wasn't until I got home that I got to see the race.

It was useful being in Barcelona for the demo race because it gave me a chance to get a feel for the stadium ahead of the Paralympics. And the scale of the Olympics was dazzling. It was a huge occasion. A lot of athletes, especially the Americans, would focus all their attention on getting into the demo race. Performing at the Olympics was everything to them and if they didn't make it, they wouldn't bother going to the Paras. I think that's because some of the guys still think there's a stigma attached to disabled sport. Nowadays this attitude is on the wane, but in Seoul there were twenty-two gold medals available for events on the track. There were so many classes that there would be just a handful of people in certain events, which devalued winning. The Paralympics should be about élite sport, just as the Olympics are, but some athletes felt that wasn't the case.

To get from the warm-up track to the main stadium there was a walkway, which went across the road and down into the main body of the stadium. We couldn't use that because of the number of steps so we had to go out of the stadium, across the road and try to get in with the general public. It was chaotic. A lot of the media didn't really know what was going on and were unaware that there even was a demo race. As we crossed the road an American film crew pitched up and started wanting to do interviews there and then. It was incredible. I was thinking, half an hour from now I'm going to be racing. Usually you are locked away from the public and you can focus. On this occasion we were cutting through the crowds, trying to force our way in. It wasn't the best preparation.

When the race did get under way, it was fast. I was in lane one and Connie Hansen and Jean Driscoll came across quickly. A gap opened up and I didn't know whether to try to make it up or let someone else take up the pace. Before I knew it I was at the back of the pack and that's where I stayed. I went through in about 1.55, which was way faster than anything I'd ever done before. It was a new experience. I'd never been at the back of the pack and not been able to go any quicker before. I was at maximum pace the whole way. It was a good race to be in and it taught me a lot, because most of my racing was in the T3s where the starts were slower. I didn't like being last but I couldn't have gone any faster. I was absolutely flat out. I had two days in Barcelona and then came home.

Three weeks later I was on my way back to Spain for the Paralympics. We flew out as the British team. We'd gone to Seoul in our different disability groups but now we were an athletics group, which was better. It meant we were being treated seriously and it also meant you got to know some of the other athletes.

The downside to travelling around the world to major competitions is the endless waiting around. I accept that, being a paraplegic, I need some help getting on to planes, but there never seems to be any system. On the way back from Sydney they'd taken all the wheels off the chairs because there were so many, but they hadn't tagged them. So they put out a call to the coaches asking them to go and identify frames and wheels. When a call goes out like that you know you are going to be sitting there for three hours. Everyone left us. I remember one of the medical team saying, 'I'm not a bag carrier.' I thought great, you can walk off the plane, but we're stuck.

I spend a lot of time sitting at airport information desks saying, 'Do you realise how important my chair is to me?' I usually meet someone who says, 'Yes, I bought my mother a chair and it cost £250.' They don't realise that mine cost around £3,500. They don't realise how important my wheels are to me. They are my legs. I don't want to be put in a horrible airport chair that is three feet too wide for me and where my feet don't reach the foot plates. It comes back to control and not liking it when that is taken away from me.

The team spirit was great on the way out to Barcelona. We got there in the early evening and the first thing you have to do is go through accreditation. There were 200 of us and 300 Americans, so it was obviously going to be a long job. Mum had packed me a box of Welsh cakes, so a few of us just sat down on the floor and ate them while we played cards. I have my circle of friends but, for me, going to a major games is not a social event. Once, at the World Championships in Berlin in

1994, a small group of us were told off by one of the coaches for not being sociable. I felt that was unfair. That wasn't my job. Berlin was boiling hot and we were in fairly dodgy accommodation with no air-conditioning. The last thing I wanted to do was chat to people I didn't know. Sometimes I do try, like when I've been the team captain, but I don't think I'm there to be the life and soul of the party. Some people treat it as a jolly, but that's not my way. They probably think I'm a bit aloof, but I don't care. My attitude is I can't be into what is important if I am heavily into the social side of it all. Some people are different and can manage both. But until I have finished competing, I have to focus.

When we got to the village it was dark. Our kit had been dumped at the side of the road, but there was no sign of the chairs. One of the coaches said they'd turn up in the morning, but I wasn't satisfied. 'You don't understand,' I said. My racing chair is one of the most important things in my life and I don't like being separated from it. It's just the way I am. I always try to take my crash helmet, gloves and a racing suit in my hand luggage so that, if I lose everything else, I can still compete. If I could, I'd take my racing chair on the plane with me too. Everyone's chair is different and you can only be at your best in your own. Mine's a very small one with a narrow frame. It's also one of the longest. When I'm travelling, there's a panic and tension that sets in until I find it. Eventually, we got our chairs that night, but only because a group of us got fairly bolshie and met a coach who was more sympathetic. Before the biggest thing in four years I cannot, psychologically, cope without my chair. Physically, I am sure it wouldn't do me any harm, but it's the time that I stamp my feet and get stroppy.

*

I knew I was in good shape from my heat in the 400 metres, but I instinctively knew that the final was not going to be as good. I went through exactly the same routine, but sometimes you just get a feeling before races. One of the coaches said to me, 'You're going to break the record again,' but I knew I wasn't. I could sense it. There was no pressure on me and I just felt very calm. Very occasionally, you get into that relaxed frame of mind. It happened before the final of the 100 metres in Sydney where I remember thinking, this is going to be all right. At other times you are just thinking, oh, my God, oh, my God.

It wasn't such a good race technically because the middle part was not great. But I knew I was going to win fairly early on because I was with Ingrid, who was on my outside, at 150 metres. When I crossed the line first I felt a wave of relief. It wasn't the high that I'd got from the semi-final, even though the time was under a minute again and the previous best in a Games final had been 63 seconds. Medals are important to me but I am a perfectionist and judge myself by how well I have performed as much as by where I have finished. When you are winning you don't think so much, whereas if you are losing you want to know why.

I've never had the perfect race. The closest I've ever come was in the 400 metres at Gothenburg in 2000. It was a hard quick track and I remember sitting there, watching the wind blow the flags, thinking, if I'm ever going to break the world record then it's here. Technically, every bit of the race was spot on. I felt like it was all happening in slow motion. I was in the outside lane, which I don't like because you are running scared. You can't see anyone else, so you are not in control. I knew I had to get the first 200 metres perfect. When I got to the 300 metre point, I could see two athletes, Jeff Adams and Kelly Smith, in my peripheral vision. They had both realised I was pushing really fast and were shouting at me from the side of the track. In all it felt like the race took ten minutes. Time froze. I took half a second off the world record. It was just one of those days when everything went right – head, weather, training, track.

There wasn't a lot of time to relax after winning the 400 metres in Barcelona because I was back on the track the following day for the 100 metres. It was probably my weakest event because of my start and I was up against some T4 athletes, so I knew I was at a disadvantage. I was in the lane next to Ingrid again and she got off to a good start. At the 50 metre point I was one-and-a-half lengths down on her. With 40 metres left I was still a length down. I was down almost the entire race but just pipped her on the line. The time was 17.55 seconds which broke my old world record. I knew I had to do that to beat Ingrid and my speed going through the line was 32 kilometres an hour which was fast. It was a dramatic way to win, although it caused a bit of panic among the family. Sian videos a lot of my races and has watched most of my career through a viewfinder. It means I have a big collection of dodgy quality tapes with a lot of screaming on and a very biased commentary. The 100 metres in Barcelona was another one to add to the collection.

There hadn't been heats for the 100 metres. That's often the way. Because of the sheer number of events they try to take just the top end. For women they set the standards so that only the top eight qualify. In Sydney it was so high that only six made it and we had two lanes spare. In some events the qualifying mark was 98 per cent of the world record, which was incredible. They need to sort it out. They need to look at the number of events and think how they could combine classes. Wheelchair racing went through a fairly rigorous reassessment in the early 1990s and the number of classes was cut from twelve to four, but some running classes haven't been cut in forty years.

It's hard not having that first round because you know that you can't make any mistakes. That adds to the pressure. We did have heats for the 200 metres, though, which was the next event. I won mine in a new Paralympic record and then had a five-hour break before the final. It's difficult when it's like that and you are racing again the same day. You can't do much, so you hang around or go home and have a sleep. The nerves build up. But the 200 metre final went really well. I crossed the line and had three golds. Now I just needed the 800 metres to complete the set, but I knew that was going to be easier said than done.

My plan was to go off fast because I didn't want to get boxed in. Ann Cody, an American athlete, was a quick starter so I knew it would be tough. I made the decision to go to the front from the start in an attempt to pull the sprint out of the other women. In the 800 you race in lanes until you reach a line which means you can break and move across. Ann, who was outside me, broke too early and took Tracey Lewis, a British athlete, with her. I was pretty certain that they'd gone too soon, but you are never totally sure and we kept on pushing. It was a hard race. I should have kept going, but thought it would be better to ease off in the second 200 metres and then kick again. I lost concentration and began worrying about what was going on around me instead of concentrating on myself. I kept expecting different people to come by. It came down to a sprint finish but I was tiring. Ann was outside me in lane two. I needed to kick with 150 metres to go but left it until 100 metres. I didn't have enough time to wind up to my top speed and Ann beat me by smidges.

Immediately it flashed up on the board that she'd been disqualified because she had broken too soon. It was tough on her because she hadn't realised and I did feel a bit sorry for her. The Americans put in a protest saying she hadn't known where the break line was, but it was pretty obvious. It's a big green line with a flag and an official sitting next to it. They tried all the usual stuff, while I came off and spoke to one of the team officials. I asked if it was true and he said, 'Yes, she's been DQ'd.' He knew she was out.

The protest took about forty minutes, I thought it would go my way, but you're never quite sure until you get official confirmation. During that time you can't leave what they call the international zone. I was there with the coaches of the wheelchair athletics team and we waited and waited and waited. There's an area where you get results sheets and once they are printed, that's final. Eventually, they came out and it was confirmed that Ann had been disqualified.

It was a strange feeling to win the medal without winning the race, but she broke a metre-and-a-half too early and that's a big jump. It wasn't just the wheel that crossed the line. It wasn't a borderline decision and she should have known better. The bizarre thing was Ann came to the medal ceremony. I don't know why she did that. I didn't speak to her about it but I think she just wanted to be there. I remember coming out for the presentation and looking up to the stands where she was watching. I knew she must have been feeling terrible, but I was just relieved to have got four golds. It was difficult for me too. I wanted to go up to her and say, 'I'm sorry, it's not the way I would have wanted to win,' but I didn't. It's the medal I feel most uncomfortable with and it will go down in the books as the time I finished second and still won. But at that level there is no excuse. She made a mistake and was punished for it. I think part of it was down to the fact that I went out very hard and she panicked and tried to follow me. So, in that respect, my plan worked.

After that incident Ann and I got to know each other fairly well and she has always been very accepting of what happened. She broke too early and that was it. She didn't cheat. That is a different issue altogether and it is a problem in our sport. We don't have so many problems with drugs cheats in wheelchair athletics, but we do have people who try to cheat by getting into the wrong classes. T4s pretend that they are T3s because they know they will have an advantage through their ability to start faster. The people who do the classifying have to have some medical background, whether it be as a doctor or a physio. They need to have a fair amount of knowledge about the spinal cord, too. All the competing athletes have to undergo a medical and are given a functional test, but some people try to con the assessors. Even now there are a few athletes who are borderline. It goes on more with the men because there is more money involved and people will always try to push the rules as far as they can.

I wasn't finished in Barcelona because I still had the relay to do. I hate the event and can't stand doing it but I didn't have a choice. Part of my problem with it is I don't like doing things I'm not prepared for and I knew we hadn't trained enough. We'd had some sessions leading up to the Games but maybe one or two of the athletes wouldn't turn up. Rose hardly came to any of the sessions and Tracey Lewis didn't always come. It takes so long to get the marks right in wheelchair relays that our training made a mockery of it. As it turned out, it didn't make much difference anyway because the Americans beat us by miles and set a world record that stood until 1998.

It felt great to have won four golds, but I still had some training to do because, four days after I got back, it was the Great North Run, a high-profile event offering very considerable prize money. We didn't go out and get drunk but I remember sitting on the beach with a bunch of people, drinking coffee and putting the world to rights. We'd been out the night before we came home and got back in about an hour before we were due to leave so it was chaos as we packed. It was just a case of throwing everything into bags. I wrapped my medals in toilet paper and stuffed them into a holdall. There was the usual trouble at the airport. When we got back we found out that our chairs had been left in Barcelona because there wasn't room on the plane. Ian and I were pretty miffed because we needed to train. Winning the Great North Run would pay for most of my racing for an entire year. But the team officials' attitude was the minute the Paralympics had finished, so had their responsibility. It took the edge off Barcelona, but after a lot of heated arguments, British Airways did a special search and got the chairs delivered next day. When I finally got home to Cardiff there was a big street party laid on for me which was great. The trouble was I was so late arriving that a lot of the kids, who'd been waiting patiently outside the house, had all gone to bed. There were loads of balloons and streamers and people came out and congratulated me.

Things had changed in a number of ways when I got back. Thanks largely to the efforts of Helen Rollason, the media coverage had improved a lot. There was a big media response at the airport and *Blue Peter* did a piece on the Games. Programmes had gone out on *Grandstand* and there was a section on the

Paralympics on the BBC *Sports Review of the Year*. Then I was named Welsh Sports Personality of the Year. It all began to snowball. I won the *Sunday Times* Sportswoman of the Year, which was a major breakthrough. It showed they were recognising Paralympics athletes as being at the same level as the non-disabled. I was up against Sally Gunnell and was sure that she would win. In the end she got the international award and I was sportswoman. That definitely helped raise the profile of disabled sport. It showed how things had moved on.

Things were changing in my personal life too. The relationship with my first real boyfriend, Andy, was coming to an end. I'd met Andy when we were both at Loughborough. He was in Towers too and was on the chemistry course. To start with we got on great, but that gradually changed and, to be fair, I probably wasn't very nice to him. When he came out to Barcelona with Dad and Sian, it was obvious things weren't right between us. Barcelona was incredibly important to me and I didn't want to spend long outside the village when I was there. It began to get difficult. When we got home from Spain, it was okay for a while and we just drifted along, hoping that things might change for the better. It was a serious relationship and if we'd carried on, we would have been looking at marriage. But it soon became clear that it was never going to be right. Andy is a really sweet guy, but I didn't think we were right for each other. Barcelona changed a lot of things for me and I think he saw it as me choosing athletics over him. I thought the two things could fit together, but when it comes to athletics I can be selfish. We broke up and I think a lot of it was my fault because we wanted different things. It was probably a sign of just how important my athletics was becoming to me.

I didn't bother to look for a job when I got back. It wasn't that I made a conscious decision to become an athlete, it just happened. My parents didn't push me to find a job and I didn't get a proper one until 1996, when I went to work for British Athletics. I could see how disability athletics was changing and we were going to be integrated within the main governing body for the first time. My interest in the political side of the sport grew after Barcelona. I was concerned about how athletes were treated and wanted to get involved.

I am still bothered about the issue of the treatment of athletes. They should not be treated like cannon fodder but sometimes they are. Everything comes down to the colour of your medal. But you can't afford to offend too many bronze medallists because they are the ones with the potential to turn it into gold. They are the future, not me. I don't know whether I'm paranoid about it or just too close, but I learnt a lot about respecting people from my coaches. When I joined Bridgend and was coached by Roy Anthony, the club was seriously up there and the girls he was coaching were all Welsh champions. Roy's attitude was it didn't matter if they were the best in the world or the worst. They could all be civil.

At the beginning of 1993 I took over as chairman of the Wheelchair Racing Association, which meant getting fairly heavily involved in politics, selection and organising events. Not many people appreciated the fact I was outspoken and some people treated me differently because I was only twenty-three. I argued quite hard for athletes' rights because, if you keep the athletes happy, it makes your job a lot easier. It's not a case of letting them get away with what they want, but one of thinking about how they are treated and mistreated.

The next major event for me was the 1993 World Championships in Stuttgart. It was my first World Championships demonstration race and, again, they weren't sure whether the race was going to go ahead or not. Having been at the Barcelona demo race, it was important to make it to Stuttgart but we didn't have trials this time. They just selected the top eight women from the previous eighteen months on time. I thought that was a fair way of doing it. The race itself was quite dull. Louise Sauvage wanted to break the world record and went off fast. Nobody wanted to go with her. She had a decent gap on everybody as a result and ended up breaking the record. Connie came second and I got bronze in a sprint finish.

Then something bizarre happened. After I'd finished racing a woman grabbed me and said, 'You've got to come with me.' Ian had gone off to get my day chair, so I was on my own with this woman who tried to drag me down a corridor which had a sign on the wall saying 'Doping Control'.

'No, no, I need to have my coach with me,' I said.

'You must come with me,' she insisted.

I didn't speak any German, so we had trouble communicating. She grabbed me by my top and began dragging me away. At that moment Ian, who was the team coach that year, turned up with my day chair.

'What's wrong?' he said.

'You come with me,' said the woman.

'I'm not going anywhere without Ian,' I said.

The woman was confused and we soon understood why. I was actually being taken to have make-up put on for the medal ceremony. There I was making a complete idiot of myself, screaming like a banshee at this poor woman, when all she had wanted to do was stick a bit of blusher on. It just so happened that the doping centre and make-up room were on the same corridor. I felt so embarrassed that I let them use whatever make-up they wanted. She had her revenge. I ended up with bright green eye shadow and orange lipstick. When I came out, Ian burst out laughing, and I went to the medal ceremony trying to wipe it all off. Sometimes they have little make-up packs for you and let you do it yourself, but at other times they have what can loosely be termed artists. I've since made a habit of looking at them beforehand. The woman in Stuttgart had garish make-up, so I should have known I was in trouble.

Stuttgart proved significant for me because it was there that I spoke to Jenni Banks about joining her coaching squad in Western Australia. Since 1991, Dave Williams had acted as my adviser. He helped me with the psychological side of things, but I knew I needed a coach. I stayed with Jenni until 1997 when I started using her advice and ideas to devise my own training programmes; and Ian played a bigger part in helping me from 1997 onwards.

I'd been thinking about going to the States to train at the end of 1993 and was keen on the University of Illinois, but that plan fell through because you had to be studying there. I began to think of other places and spoke to Jenni, a former Australian hockey player, during the World Championships. I'd known her since 1989 and we'd always got on well. She is an imposing 6ft 1in Aussie but she's quiet and has a good sense of humour. I'd got some money from the Winston Churchill Foundation and she said she was open to athletes coming over for three-and-a-half months and would be happy to have me.

That was the idea but things rarely go to plan. Just before I was due to go to Perth, I was making a cup of coffee in Ian's house in Redcar. I had a spasm in my leg, wobbled and spilt the coffee in my lap. I screamed because I was only wearing a pair of cotton Lycra tights and the water was boiling. I ripped off my tights and Ian threw some freezing cold water on me. Then he quickly ran a bath of ice cold water and I sat in it half dressed. I remember saying, 'Can I get out now?' and Ian just said, 'No, you have to stay in.' The water was up to my neck and I was freezing and shaking with the cold. Ian asked if he should call an ambulance, but I said I was all right because the tops of my legs were only pink and there didn't seem to be too much blistering. I sat there for fifteen minutes. Then I said, 'Right, I'm getting out now, the water's not going to make any difference.' And then, as I stood up, the skin fell off my legs. I sat back down and said to Ian, 'You'd better ring that ambulance.'

When the ambulance men arrived, I was still sitting in the bath. They brought a stretcher and wrapped a blanket around me. I'd taken my socks off and they asked Ian to find another pair because they needed to get me warm again. Of course, he couldn't find another clean pair. All he could come up with was a pair of old tennis socks that he had been out walking in. They were really grubby and I said, 'I'm not going to hospital in those.' Ian just said, 'Put the socks on.' He wasn't bothered about how good I looked. The ambulance men told me not to worry, so reluctantly I put them on and went off with Ian following behind in the car.

We went to the accident and emergency unit and they didn't believe me when I said I'd poured coffee on myself. They asked if I wanted to see the doctor on my own and kept trying to get Ian out of the room. Then they asked if I wanted to see the police. They obviously thought Ian was responsible. I said, 'I need a doctor, not a policeman.' Eventually, I did get to see a doctor and the first thing he did was ask me how I caught spina bifida. I looked at Ian and thought I really don't want to be here. I said quite sharply, 'It's congenital. That's the only way you can get it.' It was scary that he didn't know that. I wanted to be transferred to a spinal unit, to somewhere where they understood paraplegia, but they wouldn't allow it. I wasn't happy in Middlesbrough because I felt they didn't understand my condition. I wanted to go home to Rookwood, the local spinal unit, or Chepstow, the burns unit. The doctor wasn't very pleased that I was telling him he didn't know what he was doing, but I was on hardly any antibiotics and had a student nurse trying to change my dressing. I'd cut and burnt my legs so many times that I knew more about how to do it than she did.

I had second degree burns on my legs where I hadn't got into the water fast enough. I've still got some bad scars. I ended up having a row with the doctor about discharging myself, similar to the one we'd had in the medical centre in Loughborough five years earlier. In the end I said I'd take my chances. I asked for my notes and then they got really fussy and said they would sort something out with Chepstow. When we finally got there, they were under the impression that I had some very minor burns on my legs and that I could be seen as a day patient. They took me into the operating theatre, took off the bandages, took one look at my legs and said, 'These are not minor burns, are they?' Luckily, they were a great burns unit. I went into isolation for three days. They peeled the skin off my legs and dressed the wounds properly.

I said, 'Look, I'm going to Australia in just over a month.' And they said they weren't sure whether I'd be able to. Because I've got very poor circulation below my waist, my wounds heal very slowly. The top of my legs were not too bad, but the insides took a lot longer. Mum and Dad brought my hand crank to hospital so that I could still train, but there wasn't any treatment except rest. The doctors told me I wouldn't be able to go to

Australia until after Christmas, but I said, 'No, I need to be ready in two weeks.'

One day when I was in hospital, a huge bouquet of purple flowers arrived for me. I read the note and they were from Neil Kinnock. Not long before my accident, I'd done a television version of *Desert Island Discs* called *Six of the Best*. You had to choose your favourite television clips. Mine included a bit of *Blackadder*, Brian Hanrahan's famous report from the Falklands when he 'counted them out and counted them in' and the time when the relay team lost the shoe in the 4×400 metres in Tokyo. During the interview I'd mentioned that my favourite colour is purple and he obviously remembered. It was very sweet of him.

I did make it to Australia on schedule, although the doctors told me to stay out of the sun – quite hard considering where I was going! At the airport Mum was fairly emotional. Whenever I went off competing, she always used to say to me, 'Well, it's not as if it's the other side of the world.' But this time it was. I'd been there before, but never for this length of time and I was going to be away for Christmas. We sat in the airport having a drink, not saying very much to each other and studying the incoming fights. I glanced at Mum and saw that she was crying.

I lived with Louise Sauvage and her family. I knew Lou quite well and I trained with her, Jen and a couple of other athletes. We trained ten times a week. It was no holiday – early morning, mid-afternoon, Sundays off! It rained twice while I was there and we lived near the beach and went swimming a lot. It was great. During my time there, I realised Australia is much better than Britain at co-ordinating disability training. There was also a lot more media coverage of wheelchair sport, and events were better integrated into the non-disabled track and field pro-gramme. It provided a lot of food for thought.

At the end of my time in Oz we went to Los Angeles for the marathon. I got there ahead of the Aussie athletes and found the hotel. It had a glamorous name but was disgusting. I'd never seen anything like it. There were prostitutes and a guy selling drugs standing outside. Cigarette burns dotted the sheets. I didn't want to go out of the room because it was so dodgy but I didn't want to stay in there either. An hour later the Aussies arrived. I went outside to greet them and said to Jen, 'You're never going to believe this place.'

'Why, is it really nice?' she asked.

She soon got her answer. We stayed one night because we didn't have a car and it was late, but as soon as the car hire places opened, we were out of there and off to find somewhere better. And then I broke the toilet in the new place and flooded it when I tried to fix it. I wasn't very popular. The LA Marathon didn't go very well either, but I came home with lots of good memories of my time in Australia. It was a great experience and there was a real bond between the athletes.

My world had changed. I was number one in the world and would stay there until 1996. Barcelona had opened a lot of doors and had raised my profile to new heights. I always considered myself as plain old Tanni the athlete. Now I realised other people saw me differently. I had to get used to the fact that four gold medals had turned me into a celebrity. Other people had been through a similar experience. Daniela for instance was idolised at home in Switzerland and we spoke about fame and the atten-tion. I really valued Daniela's advice. She was a true friend and rival which is why it was such a shock when I heard some dreadful news in 1994.

I was at home in Cardiff when Mum took a call from Chris Cohen, one of the technical officers from the British team. She said I was to ring him back straightaway, so I did. I instantly knew something awful had happened.

'Hello, Tanni, I'm afraid I've got some bad news.' I felt my heart sink. 'Daniela's been killed.'

'What?'

'I'm sorry, she was hit by a car while out training.'

I came off the phone and Mum was standing in the doorway. I looked at her, tears streaming down my face, and said, 'Daniela's dead.'

I was traumatised by the news. I felt helpless but I had to do something, so I started leafing through my diary and ringing other athletes on the circuit to tell them.

Not long afterwards I was at an airport in Germany and I saw Daniela's face on the front of *Swiss Illustrated*. I picked up the magazine and flicked to a double-page spread of her accident scene. There was an ambulance on the left-hand side, people walking around the wreckage of the chair and, worst of all, a body bag on the floor. I sat in the newsagent's in the airport and cried.

Daniela's death had a profound effect on me. If she'd been two minutes later pushing up the road she might still be here today. Only a few months later an American athlete, whom I had met a few times, was killed while training on the roads. Those incidents highlighted the dangers of the sport. Daniela was killed just after the World Championships in 1994. Later that week a demonstration event was due to be held at the European Championships in Helsinki. My season had been good and I was expecting to win because I'd done well at the Worlds. There was some discussion among the athletes about what we should do, even to the point of whether we should compete or not. I honestly believe Daniela would have wanted us to carry on and we received a message from her family saying something similar. But things just seemed to get worse. The funeral was held on the day of the race. Lily Angrenny was so upset that she made black armbands for us all to wear. We were told that they were going to make an announcement about Daniela during the medal ceremony, but when we were on the start line there was a long delay while the announcer explained why there was an empty lane. A photograph was taken of me on the line, and it has been used extensively. I look focused and serious, which is not how I remember feeling. What I do recall is that the emotion flooded through me and the race was a bit of a blur. I wasn't sharp, didn't push that well and made some stupid tactical decisions. I couldn't sprint for the line and came third. In the whole scheme of things it didn't matter very much. It proves that sometimes, just sometimes, there are more important things than winning.

Chapter Six

Does She Take Sugar?

WHAT'S it like being disabled? That's probably the one question I get asked more than any other. People think I must have overcome enormous obstacles to be a success as an athlete, but I don't see it like that at all. A journalist from the *Guardian*, whom you might have expected to know better, said to me recently, 'It must be really tragic being in a wheelchair.' My first reaction was it must be really tragic working for the *Guardian*. I actually have a very fulfilling life. I don't think of myself as disabled but I know I am lucky. Athletics has changed things for me dramatically and as I have become more well known, people's attitudes towards me have changed. But there are still a lot of issues that need addressing and there is an awful lot of prejudice and ignorance about disability. It's a taboo subject. People don't like it, so they shove it under the carpet.

Like most disabled people, I have come up against the 'does-she-take-sugar?' syndrome on a few occasions. Because I am in a chair some people assume I am mentally subnormal and treat me like dirt. On one occasion when that happened I was shopping in Birmingham. I went to the counter with a skirt and held it out with my credit card. There were two girls behind the counter and they categorically refused to look at me. I wasn't in a hurry, so I decided to conduct an experiment. I thought I would wait there without saying anything and see how long it took one of them to acknowledge me. So I waited as they kept sweeping their eyes over me. Another shopper came along and they served her straightaway while I just sat there and suffered in silence. The minutes passed and it seemed as if I was there for hours. I could feel my blood boiling up inside me. Then a third assistant came along and said, 'Are you waiting to be served?'

'No, I'm waiting for a bus actually.' She looked at me quite strangely, so I said, 'Yes, I am waiting to be served and I have been for six minutes.'

'What happened?' she asked.

'Your assistants seemed to want to ignore my presence.'

'Well, you should have said something.'

That did it.

'I thought the fact I was sitting here holding a skirt and a credit card might actually signify that I wanted to buy something,' I said sharply.

And then one of the other girls piped up. 'I was waiting for your carer to come back.'

I was seething by this point. I have a really bad temper and try not to lose it. If Ian loses his temper he can be frighteningly controlled and is very cutting and rational. I just explode and become a complete raving lunatic. I glared at this girl and said, 'Why should you presume I have a carer?'

She stuttered and stumbled and then spluttered, 'Well, you're in a wheelchair, aren't you?'

Then another of them, wearing a big inane grin on her face, said, 'Would you like to buy the skirt anyway?'

'No, not any more,' I said and swept out. I was livid and went home and wrote a letter to the store's head office. They sent me lots of gift vouchers in return, but I just ripped them up and sent them back with a curt note. It said: 'For the amount of money you spend on customer service, there is obviously a deficiency in your disability awareness training. Any person who comes into your shop would expect to receive a much better standard of service. Thank you very much but I will never use your shop again.'

To this day I haven't set foot inside any of their stores. I only use chain stores that are easily accessible. They can afford to be and I'm only going to spend money in those shops if they want me. It's different when it comes to the small independent shops, but they tend to have better service anyway. There is a little kitchen shop in Cardiff that is not particularly accessible, but they will help me. If I say I'd like a potato peeler they will go and get one for me. The daft thing is the big chains are missing out. The statistics show that disabled people can have a large amount of disposable income, but they are not going to spend it unless they are treated as valued customers.

On another occasion Ian and I went for a meal in a restaurant. I asked for the bill and when they brought it they gave it to Ian. Part of that might have been a male–female thing, but it was more likely a disability issue. Then I signed it in the wrong place and the waiter said to Ian, 'Can you get her to sign it there?'

Ian just ignored him and said, 'Tanni, I think someone's speaking to you.' That's his way of dealing with it.

When we go out, people often assume he is my carer because, although he is a wheelchair athlete, Ian can walk with a stick. He is more touchy about it than I am. I think that's because he broke his back when he was twenty-one, whereas I have never known anything different. I don't think of Ian as being disabled. Okay, it takes him slightly longer to get up the stairs, but it's never affected him in the sense of stopping him from doing anything he wants to do. People like to know how you become disabled though, and I am the same. The guys in wheelchair racing are usually in it because they have done something very spectacular like breaking their neck while diving off the coast of Thailand, or something very mundane like crashing a bike outside their house. I want to know what happened to them. I am as curious as the next person, but I wouldn't ask a lot of the questions people throw at me.

People can be very personal and quite rude and think nothing of it. For example, echoing my mother's concern, I am often asked, 'Can you have a baby?' Once I was doing an interview for *Woman's Realm* and the journalist asked, 'Can you have a normal sex life?' I thought, woah there, where did that come from? I mean, what is normal anyway? Another favourite question is, 'How do you go to the toilet?' When I go into schools, I don't have a problem with kids asking those questions. They can't quite get their heads round the whole wheelchair thing, but you would have thought adults might have a better comprehension. I try to be patient. I know people are only asking because they want to know more about disability but when one person asked me how I went to the toilet, I remember saying, 'Well, how do you do it?' That shut her up.

Kids are just very blunt and inquiring, whereas adults sometimes make things worse by trying too hard to treat you normally. Once, I fell out of my chair while rushing to get somewhere in Birmingham. I was carrying a stack of paper and wasn't looking where I was going. I fell into a puddle of mushy leaves and the contents of my bag went flying. There I was, flapping around on the floor like a dying fish, when I noticed a man looking at me. It was as if it was an everyday experience to see a person sprawled on the floor like that. Then he must have realised who I was because he came over to me.

'You're Tanni Grey,' he said.

'That's right,' I said, trying to hide my embarrassment. And he proceeded to talk to me in depth about the Paralympics and the London Marathon and Birmingham hosting the World Championships. I was nodding and scrambling around like an idiot, picking up two pence pieces as he carried on.

Then he said, 'Right, I'd better be off,' and he left me there, lying on the floor in a puddle. It was odd, but I think it was probably down to the fact he didn't know what to do. People are like that a lot. They don't know how to react around disabled people and feel embarrassed.

The answer is to treat disabled people as you would anyone else. I don't like it when people pat me on the head but I don't think anybody would like that. Unfortunately, some people just can't help behaving in a way that offends. When I went to the Commonwealth Games in 1994, one official introduced me as 'my little friend'. Then, at a reception for the officials, they were doing these daft military songs, complete with marching actions. One bloke asked me how I pushed my chair, so I showed him and then they all started doing these pushing motions instead. I am sure it was done with the best of intentions, but it just made me mad. I left the reception early.

Perhaps the one episode that has said most about attitudes to disability in this country in recent times has been the Glenn Hoddle affair. On 29 January 1999 I knew nothing about Glenn

Hoddle apart from the fact he was the England football manager. Twenty-four hours later I had given twenty-two interviews about him. It was incredible.

It all started when I was sitting in an Indian restaurant in Birmingham with Martin Corck, my agent, and my mobile phone rang. It was Ian, who hadn't been able to join us because he was working. He said Radio Five Live wanted to speak to me first thing the following morning. I asked him what it was about and he said Glenn Hoddle. I couldn't understand why anyone would want to speak to me about football, but it became clearer by the time I got home. The radio station had faxed through a transcript of an interview with Glenn Hoddle that was going to be printed in *The Times* the following day. It was largely about football but he made some comments about his belief in reincarnation and disabled people. People interpreted it as him saying the disabled were paying for sins committed in past lives. I spoke to Martin and Ian about what I should say. I wanted to get it clear in my own head what I thought, because journalists are good at manipulating your words and taking bits of quotes out of context. Ian's opinion was that they wanted to get rid of Hoddle as the England manager and this was what they were going to use to do it. It was the stick they were going to beat him with.

The following morning I did the interview on Radio Five Live. It was 6 a.m. and I really didn't want to be awake at that time because I was due to be at Alsager College near Crewe that morning for sports science testing. I still had no concept about how big this story was becoming and thought the interview was on so early because they didn't have anything else to fill the slot. I figured nobody would be listening at that time anyway. There was someone from a disability group on too, to give a more political view, and I think they were expecting at least one of us to slag him off for his comments. But both of us said that it was difficult to know from the article what the context had been. My reading of the story was that he was just talking about his belief in reincarnation. He wasn't saying that if you are a disabled person you were evil. It was what you had done in past lives. If you believe in reincarnation and the whole Karma system, that is what you will believe. What you sow, you reap. I don't believe that myself and am not a particularly religious person. I have no interest in Glenn Hoddle's spiritual beliefs, but the bottom line was Glenn Hoddle wasn't being abusive to disabled people.

The other woman on the programme was saying the same things and I could sense the interviewer getting frustrated because we weren't sticking the boot in. They were dying for us to crucify him, but our opinion was it was no big deal. I thought there are far more important things to worry about in society than a few throwaway words from some football manager. I think my parting comment was, 'If you want to get rid of him as a football manager, do it because he's not a very good one, not because of something he may or may not have said.'

I thought that would be that, but the rest of that day went completely mad. The phone never stopped ringing. I did *The Times*, the *Sun*, the *Daily Mail*, the *Daily Telegraph* and the *Daily Express*. Gary Lineker did a live phone interview with me on *Grandstand* and Sky sent a huge juggernaut with a fifteen-foot satellite on top to this little college in Alsager. My policy is that if someone can be bothered to ask me for an interview I always try to give them one, but that day was absolutely mental. And the trouble with most of the interviews was that I wasn't saying what they wanted me to say. Anyway, it was a football story rather than a disability one. I remember thinking where were all the people who are so upset about Glenn Hoddle when the Disability Discrimination Act (DDA) was being put into place? Why weren't they speaking out for an equal rights act, like they have in America, instead of all the different acts we have here?

I was a member of the National Disability Council between 1996 and 1999 because I was keen to make sure the DDA was implemented properly. I thought I could contribute to that but I didn't think the act was all it should have been. In America they have a civil rights act so everybody is equal. Here you are considered normal if you are white, male and middle-class and then there are a host of acts to deal with those who are not considered normal – women, ethnic minorities and the disabled. In America everybody begins at the same starting point. The DDA gave people more opportunity but it was too long-term. It said things like transport had to be sorted out within ten years. In America that would have been sorted out overnight.

A lot of people were very outspoken about Glenn Hoddle, but what have they done since then to move forward the focus on disability and improve the lives of the majority of disabled people in the United Kingdom? The fact is a lot of them have done nothing. I have been fortunate to have had a good education, good parents and now I have the money to be able to make choices, but the reality is that life for a disabled person costs a lot more than it does for the non-disabled. You need lifts, aids, chairs and are far less likely to be in employment or receive higher education. There are still plenty of places where you cannot go. Your choices about were you live and where you are educated are far more limited than for someone who is walking around on two feet and is perceived as normal. All these things make the life of a disabled person more difficult. And the fact is there is still a huge amount of discrimination against disabled people in the United Kingdom. A lot of disabled children grow up accepting it because they have never known anything different and believe that is just the way society is. They almost believe that is the way they should be treated. Kids with congenital diseases don't even realise when they are being discriminated against because they have grown up in a culture where that happens on a daily basis – from being barred from joining a sports club to not being allowed mainstream education and failing to get jobs. If you are treated like that all the time, you don't realise that you can be treated differently.

In those few days when the Glenn Hoddle story was front-page news, a lot of people jumped on the bandwagon. I remember David Mellor saying how terrible Glenn Hoddle was and how dare he say those things. A couple of weeks beforehand I'd been at a dinner where David Mellor had said, 'You are all so brave and wonderful.' I found that very condescending. I said on *Grandstand* that this debate should set an agenda for what we are doing for disabled people in the United Kingdom and what society is doing to make life better for everybody. What it ended up being was a three-day story and then everybody forgot about it. The acres of newspaper reports soon became fish and chip wrappers. You hoped it would help change people's attitudes about disability, but it didn't do that at all. The media just used it in a fairly opportunist manner. As soon as he had been forced to go, they moved on to something else. And everybody forgot about these 'poor disabled people' who were supposed to have been so insulted by Glenn Hoddle.

I wasn't surprised when he resigned but I was sorry that they didn't have the guts to sack him because the England footballers weren't very good. Mind you, I find that whole concept strange anyway. You have eleven players on a pitch getting paid a fortune and they never get the blame for performing badly. If I race badly, it is my fault. Full stop.

That spate of interviews brought up the disability vocabulary issue. Interviewers are always putting their foot in it. I have words and phrases that I dislike more than others. I don't like handicapped because it comes from cap in hand and implies begging. I consider myself a person with a disability not a disabled person, and I am not confined to a wheelchair. The phrase 'disability athletics' automatically puts the focus on the disability rather than the athlete, so I don't like that, and I hate being called a wheelie because it puts the emphasis on the chair and not me. I'd rather be called a gimp than that. It is all about being treated in a fair and equitable manner.

A lot of people are still quite ignorant. One of my worst experiences came when I was travelling to Australia to take up my Winston Churchill fellowship. I'd paid £870 for my ticket with Cathay Pacific and then the airline told me that I'd have to pay for someone else to accompany me because I was a wheelchair-user. I'd flown all over the world but that was the first time anyone had said that. What made it more annoying was they had cashed my cheque a month earlier and they initially said I'd have to pay a 10 per cent cancellation fee if I wanted to try other airlines. Even the booking form was offensive because it asked if my disability would cause offence to other passengers.

In the end I got the European director grovelling to me on the phone, but he just made things worse. At one point he said, 'people like you'. I said, 'What do you mean – Welsh? Brown eyes? Dark hair?'

'I'm sorry,' he gushed. 'If I'd realised the consequences, I would never have suggested you needed to take someone else.'

'Are you saying you did what you did because you thought you could get away with it?' I asked.

The more he tried to apologise, the more he dug himself into a bigger hole. I eventually flew out with British Airways. I got a full refund from Cathay Pacific but have never used them since.

That is all part of what it's like to be disabled. But the truth is I do not have the typical life of a disabled person. As my profile began to rise steadily after Barcelona, my life became easier in many ways. People started to recognise me as an athlete rather than a disabled person.

I don't consider myself famous but I started to become aware that other people did view me as a celebrity. I suppose I realised I was seen in that way when *Hello!* magazine rang me up and said they wanted to come and photograph me at home in Birmingham, which was where I had gone to work for British Athletics in 1996. I was amazed that they would be interested, but I thought it would be a laugh so I agreed. Before they came I tidied up big time. I made sure the house was absolutely immaculate. When the photographer turned up he wasn't particularly impressed. I suppose it was not as palatial as the pads of the famous he was used to. But there I was, in my little two-bedroomed house in Birmingham, with a few pages devoted to me instead of Tom Cruise or Julia Roberts. My friends all thought it was brilliant and rushed out to buy copies of the magazine.

When *Hello!* asked if they could do our wedding, both Ian and I were initially unsure but we agreed. We got married in Cardiff at my parents' church and had to go down a pedestrianised area to get there. There were hundreds of people milling around and

I said to Dad, 'There are a lot of people in Cardiff today. There must be something happening.' Then it dawned on me that they were there to watch me get out of the car. It was lovely but it was a shock. I'll read the gossip columns like the next person, but if someone really famous was getting married down the road, I don't think I'd make the effort to go and watch.

It's odd being considered a celebrity. People see only a tiny little bit of me, but that is enough to make you public property. Competing is one small facet of my life. Real life is going on the treadmill in my garage in the morning, doing the washing-up and going to the supermarket. A lot of people stop me and want to talk to me which is great and 99 per cent of them are really nice. They just want to say hello. I was in a Somerfield supermarket once and a woman started chatting to me about Sydney and how she'd watched it all on the television. Then she turned to her husband and said, 'She doesn't look as good in real life does she?' I thought, you wouldn't either if you'd just been on a sixteen-mile run, but she wasn't being nasty. It's just that people feel they can say what they like because they feel they know you.

I find the whole fame thing very curious and it comes back to what I said earlier about not being in awe of anyone myself. When I go to the Sports Personality programme at the BBC, I do go, 'God, there's Muhammad Ali' and 'God, there's the entire Manchester United football team', but I know they are just normal people. I was at a dinner one night and one of the actors from *Brookside* was there. His wife came over to me and said, 'My husband would really like to meet you, but he's too shy to come over.' I was staggered. He was more famous than I was!

I like being in the public eye and I can't imagine there is an athlete who does not enjoy celebrity status. It's part of the reason you do it in the first place. All we are really doing is showing off and you need that ego to be able to put yourself on the line and compete. There are pros and cons to being in the spotlight. I am always careful about what I say to the media, which probably comes from my politics background, but I'm not fed up with that yet. I have never been badly misquoted and the press I get is not very intrusive and is generally positive. I am sure it would be different if I was Posh Spice and they were criticising me for what I was wearing every day, but luckily it's not like that.

I know that the press can be useful in helping to raise the profile of disability sport and the wider issue of disabled rights. But I don't think I have any right to put myself forward as a spokesperson for the disabled because I don't have to endure many of the problems many people encounter. I try to stay clear of being used as a figurehead, but I think it does do some good to see disabled people doing well on television and in the papers. How much good is debatable. David Blunkett is very much in the public arena but I'm not sure that has changed people's attitude to visual impairment. I think there are two sides to it. You need to have examples of disabled people in the public eye, but you also need campaigners. I've never been a campaigner myself, and have never been into chaining myself to railings, but the two things together can help bring about change.

The first thing to do is admit that people are frightened by disability. I think that disabled people have been segregated in society for so long that the non-disabled are not used to them and are uncomfortable with the whole idea. For a long time in this country, disabled children were just left to die. They weren't given treatment at birth or there wasn't the medical technology to keep them alive. If I'd been born twenty years earlier, I probably wouldn't have lived. That is the ultimate segregation. With the improvements in medical technology, things are a lot better now than they were. But people are being discriminated against every single day and, while I have not experienced much of it myself, we all need to accept that there is still a long way to go.

Chapter Seven

An American
Nightmare

I FIRST met Ian Thompson at a training weekend in 1986 and thought he was a fairly obnoxious individual. He overheard me saying I was going to Loughborough and he made some quip about it being a PE college and not a proper university. I wasn't terribly impressed. We didn't get on badly but we didn't get on well. My memories of that first meeting are mainly of him being very rude to me, making fun of my training and saying how politics wasn't a real degree subject and I should be doing something like maths or science. But as time went on I got to know him better and realised he was a nice guy. A lot of athletes don't like passing information on to other athletes. They feel a bit threatened, but Ian always had time to help others and was very patient with me.

He never really asked me out and we just sort of drifted into it. We saw each other a lot at competitions and training weekends and when I was upset about my break-up with Andy, he proved a very good listener. I also realised we had the same, slightly sarcastic, sense of humour. We grew closer throughout 1993 and 1994, but it was never the most romantic of relationships. We have never gone round holding hands, being lovey-dovey or whispering sweet nothings in each other's ears. He lived in Redcar and I was a six-hour drive away in Cardiff, but I didn't want to move in with him because I didn't want him supporting me. He would have been happy to do that, but I didn't have a job so we stuck with our long-distance relationship.

Everything we did was centred on training and competing. Ian motivated me in different ways – by gently encouraging me, moaning that I wasn't trying hard enough and shouting at me. He also helped me a lot with my technique. Being a wheelchair athlete too means he understands a lot of what I am going through (and vice versa). He's good for me because he knows how my mind works and when to say things and when to keep quiet.

In August 1994 I found myself in the position of being Ian's team manager at the Commonwealth Games in Victoria. There was an exhibition race at the Games for men but nothing for women so, when the English wheelchair athletics team said they needed someone to fly out as a manager and my name got put forward by the Wheelchair Racing Association, I thought, why not? It meant wearing English team kit which caused quite a lot of mickey-taking from the Welsh men's team, but that would prove to be the least of my concerns.

There were quite a few people who were not happy with the fact that I was going as team manager. One of them was high up in the Commonwealth Games Council for England. I took a call from him one day and was staggered by his attitude.

'You can't go to Canada as the team manager because you are a woman and a wheelchair-user,' he said.

'Will you put that in writing?' I asked.

'I'd be glad to.'

I was told by his office that he did not mean to be patronising but was just concerned about my ability to do the job. I felt that as a disabled athlete myself I would have a good understanding of the athletes' needs. They also needed someone who understood the international technical rules and I fitted that bill too. But the message from on high was very clear. I rang the British Paralympic Association (BPA) immediately but they were not particularly supportive and told me not to rock the boat. Someone even said I was just angling for a free trip to Canada. That wasn't the case at all. I'd been to Canada loads of times and I knew this would be no holiday. Athletes can be a huge pain and always want things done two hours ago. It's not a lot of fun being an official and the intimation that I was looking for a freebie was very annoying. I rang Pete Carruthers, who had been the one who'd put my name forward, and explained the situation and the BPA's attitude.

'Right,' he said. 'Whatever else we're going to do, Tanni, you are coming to Victoria. That's what we're fighting for now.' Since 1988 wheelchair athletics had always been run by disabled athletes, so I found it difficult to understand why they were so anti me. But with the athletes' backing I did go on the trip as team manager.

If I thought that was the end of the problems I was wrong. During the Games a high-ranking Australian official, Norman Tunstall, came out with lots of comments against disabled athletes, saying they had no right to be at the Commonwealth Games. I met the press officer for the English team that day and she said, 'When you go training and the journalists start contacting you, don't say anything.'

I wanted to find out exactly what Tunstall had said so I went to the team headquarters where there were banks of fax machines so you could send messages to athletes. I said to one of the girls on the desk that I was looking for Jenni Banks, who was with the Australian team, and she said, 'Oh, yeah, and I know why.'

'I'm not having a go,' I said. 'I just want to find out what was really said. I don't want to blast the guy before I've even seen his comments.'

I got in touch with Jen and she told me what he'd said. It was pretty inane stuff. He was just another person who didn't understand that we actually train as hard as non-disabled athletes. That's the bit that annoys me. People assume anyone could sit in a wheelchair and suddenly do a marathon in an hour and a half. But if you put someone like Steve Redgrave, who's a pretty strong bloke, in a chair, he wouldn't cope. It would take him two years of training and perfecting his technique before he would be able to compete and, even then, he wouldn't win. When I came back from Barcelona with four gold medals one journalist asked me if I trained! That's the attitude we have to try to change. Tunstall was just another bloke with prejudices.

Some of the English team were fairly offhand with me, too. I remember I went into the team office one day to check the mail box for information about the day's schedule. A girl behind the desk said to me in a pretty dismissive voice, 'I suppose you want the mail.'

'Yes,' I said. 'If that's okay.'

Then in walked Linford Christie and everybody swarmed around him and started treating him like royalty. I'd met Linford before, during the BBC's *Children In Need*. He saw me, took me by the hand and gave me a huge hug and a kiss. 'Ah, Miss Grey,' he said. 'How are you?'

I tried to sound as cool as he was, despite being annoyed. 'Er fine, Linford. How are you?' That incident helped. People started treating me better and attitudes slowly changed as people became more accepting. The attitude of mainstream athletes has always been pretty good, but some of the technical staff have taken a little longer to catch up. I felt some headway was made in Victoria in terms of changing perceptions and the ice eventually broke as more people understood what we do. I ended up staying in the men's block with the cyclists, swimmers, boxers and the wheelchair racing team. One day one of the boxers was sitting outside trying to sew his support back together. He was struggling so much that I offered to do it for him. Not that I am a great stitcher but we have to sew rubber on to our pushrims on our chairs and I have fairly tough fingers for it. As a thank you Ian Irwin, the boxing coach, went out and bought me a box of chocolates.

I enjoyed being with the guys. As well as Ian, there was only Dave Holding, Jack McKenna and Ivan Newman in the team and I'd go training with them. Some people thought I shouldn't be doing that, but it was horrible being at a major event like Victoria and not competing. There was lots of administrative stuff to do and that was pretty dull and frustrating. I wished I could be out on the track.

After the Games, the support for the athletes was very positive and we were actually told that 'everything worked perfectly'. Tunstall's comments, too, had a positive effect in the same way that the ramp incident at the BBC did. It got us in the news and raised the profile. It also made people think about how we should be included in future. Up until that point, mainstream athletics didn't know where we fitted in and we had no relationship at all with the AAA of England or the British Athletics Federation.

As Ian and I became closer, from 1993 onwards, we both began focusing on going to Atlanta. I'm the one who gets all the publicity but Ian is a very good racer too. He's in the top three to five in Britain and is the British record-holder for the 5000 metres, but there are an awful lot more men competing, so it's harder to get to the very top. By 1994 I already had one eye on Atlanta but there were other things to occupy my thoughts first. The main target in 1994 was the World Championships, which are held every four years. This time they were in Berlin and, in some ways, they were disappointing. Nobody came to watch, so it was really quiet with no atmosphere. I was sharing a room with Yvonne Holloway, a British T4 athlete, in a huge concrete tower block in East Germany. It was a bit grim with no grass anywhere and the heat was so bad that a number of athletes became dehydrated. But on the track they were a great championships for me. I won golds in the 100, 200, 400 and 800 metres, the bronze in the 10,000 metres and broke the 200 and 400 metres world records. Those championships would also be the last time I competed against Ingrid Lauridsen, as she retired that year. She had been my strongest rival and we had been at so many events together that it was odd when she was no longer there. Ingrid was a determined character who spoke fluent German, French and English and her retirement marked the end of an era. It was strange to think she would not be at Atlanta in two years' time but, by then, there would be a new precocious talent for me to have to contend with.

Through 1995 and 1996 I was still ranked number one in the world and everything was geared towards peaking for the Paralympics. I planned my year around it. I went to the demonstration race at the mainstream World Championships in Gothenburg in 1995 and was the only T3 to make it. There was a fantastic atmosphere in the stadium and the track was really fast. I came fourth and people kept asking me if I was disappointed, but I wasn't. I couldn't have gone any quicker and I knew that I had no chance of winning because I was up against T4s. It was another good race for me and my plans were progressing nicely. But the atmosphere was soon to change and the build-up to the Paralympics would become dominated by arguments, accusations and bitterness.

At Barcelona, athletes with learning disabilities had been excluded and they had their own Games in Madrid instead. But shortly afterwards it was decided that there would be a limited programme for them in Atlanta. Ian and I were part of a group of athletes who were quite vocal against the inclusion of athletes with learning disabilities. We weren't against the athletes themselves but our argument was that learning difficulty (LD) sport didn't have a proper classification system. We had to be medically, functionally and sportingly classified, but in the LD classes you just had to find two people who would vouch for you and say that you had a learning difficulty. We wanted to be seen as élite athletes, not people just having a go. Sport in the UK needed to look at the best opportunity for athletes. Many athletes with LD compete to a very high level in mainstream sport, and that threw in to question some of the people who competed in disability events. It was quite an emotive argument. One official said to us that he believed that LD athletes should have the opportunity to compete at Special Olympics, Paralympics and the Olympic Games, depending on the level of performance that they reached. To us the Paralympics are élite and very few others get the opportunity to chose. Special Olympics are generally for those with Downs Syndrome and focus on participation. Everyone who takes part gets a medal.

The Paralympics had made a lot of progress and we were beginning to be accepted as sportsmen and women in our own right. We both felt that expansion of the Games was positive but it also had to be weighed up carefully against the number of events on the programme. Partial inclusion is not a particularly fair method. If you let some sports in you had to let the lot in. At the moment the number of classes can be a bit confusing to people on the outside. Part of the refinement of the Games is to look at how to make the sporting spectacle more understandable to the general public.

The trouble was it was such an emotive issue that it was easy to turn the argument against us and portray us in a bad light. The people who wanted the LD athletes in accused us of being discriminatory and plain nasty. They said our only concern was that people would think it was Special Olympics. That wasn't the case at all, but it became a huge issue. We were on a non-winner from the start and Ian and I were publicly taken apart in the lead-up to Atlanta because we were asked our opinions and we gave them. We didn't have a problem with LD athletes, but we did with the way their sport was classified.

It was against the background of that ongoing argument that I went to Atlanta for the Olympic wheelchair racing demonstration race. If I was glad to get away from the arguing, I soon realised there were going to be other problems at the Games. I went to the holding camp in Tallahasse and it was there that I started hearing stories and interviews with athletes saying how difficult conditions were at the Olympics. Ian couldn't take the time off to come with me before the Paras, so a friend of mine, Mark Bullock, came with me. Bollo is one of the tennis coaches and a good mate. I wanted someone with me whom I knew well and who had been to a major games before. Bollo brought his bike out so that he could come training with me and we began to pick up a lot of bad vibes about what was going on in Atlanta.

However, nothing could have prepared us for what happened next.

Bollo and I were watching television one night and moaning about the sports coverage in America, saying how it wasn't like the good old BBC, when there was a news flash. BOMB EXPLODES IN OLYMPIC VILLAGE flashed across the bottom of the screen. We sat stunned for a second and then Bollo said, 'God, I hope the rest of the team's okay.' We both rang home to say we were fine. Even though we were a long way from the actual bomb, we knew our families would be worried. I never thought the Olympics wouldn't go ahead in the aftermath and I wasn't worried about my own safety, but when we flew to the Olympic village the security was incredible. There were loads of police at the airport with guns and sniffer dogs. When we went through for accreditation we had to have an X-ray done of our hands. This was to be used to get in and out of the Olympic village. It was very high tech and Bollo joked that it was like something out of *Star Trek*.

But when we got to the village we found it was very different. I couldn't use my hand print to get through the turnstiles so they let me in and out of side gates without checking my ID. That was a bit worrying, although I tend to have a fairly naive view of things and just believe it will be okay. I'd been to Atlanta three years before and had gone out training in a very dodgy area of town full of drug dealers. I waved to them and said hello and they waved back. When I got back to the hotel the concierge had a go at me for going off on my own into what was known to be a bad area. Then everyone at reception joined in and finally the hotel manager came out and warned me not to go there again. But I'd been fine. My theory is that if I see people who look a bit dodgy near where I'm training I make a point of saying hello and being nice to them. That way they're less likely to do anything!

There was one guy at the Olympic village who *was* taking his security duties very seriously. I often stop and chat to people around the village because it is interesting and they can often help you. So one day I found myself talking to this Vietnam veteran who was a police officer.

'They bussed me in from a couple of states away and I'm living in a trailer park,' he said.

'Is it okay?'

'Not bad, ma'am,' he said. 'Now you don't have to worry about a thing with me here. If anyone tries anything I'll shoot them.'

'Right.'

'If I'd been there when the bomb went off, I tell you I'd have shot the lot of them.'

It was then that I realised I was talking to Rambo. In his own way, he was very sweet and he would have defended the British team to the death, but who knows how many people he'd have killed in the process? I just smiled. You can't really say to an armed nutcase, 'Excuse me, are you sane?' Luckily, Bollo came along at that point and he rescued me. I came fourth in the race and wasn't sorry to be leaving Atlanta.

While I didn't find conditions at the Olympics that bad, I knew that it was bound to be worse for the Paralympics and my fears were justified when I flew out to Pensacola to the Paralympic holding camp. We were staying at a navy training college and it was not very suitable for disabled athletes. It was the first time the BPA had organised something like that and they learnt a lot from the experience. The idea was to bring people together before moving on to the Paralympic village, but there were a lot of problems with accessibility and some of the guys in wheelchairs couldn't even get into their bathrooms.

I had to go to Atlanta before the others on the team because I was having my classification checked. I went to see two physios who prodded me around a bit and tested my functions. Like doping, it's random selection and it's not happened to me very often. Unfortunately, the system is open to abuse. You also get classified by your country and it's obviously in their interests to have you in your best event. That can lead to some countries bending the rules and trying to get you in different categories from the one in which you should be competing.

We were staying in what had been the Olympic village but it was being pulled down all around us. Rambo had gone and security was a lot more lax. As soon as the Olympics were over they moved in and ripped out the dining hall. We went to the stadium and the media tent and the electronic timing devices had all gone. Olympic Park, where they had lots of stalls selling kit and souvenirs, had been closed down by the time we arrived. Their attitude was that the Olympics were done and dusted. The Atlanta Braves stopped playing their baseball games during the Games, but as soon as they were over they resumed. The Paralympics seemed like an afterthought. The American media wasn't remotely interested in the Games. Nothing comes close to Monday night football and basketball over there.

And the accommodation wasn't great either. We were in apartments with four bedrooms, two bathrooms and a little living area. There were kitchens but the fridges didn't work and the oven doors had been glued up. Then the toilets flooded and at certain times of the day, there would be no water. I was sharing with Nicola Jarvis. We got on really well, which was a good job because once we were both in the room she couldn't get by me to get out!

The Americans seemed to think everything was fine, but maybe it's easier to blind yourself to what other people think when it is your own country. There were a lot of things that didn't help you to settle. I had to queue two-and-a-half hours for my first meal and our accommodation was at the bottom of a steep hill. It took a long time to push up and down and a lot of athletes suffered shoulder problems at the Games as a result. Pushing in a day chair is a completely different action from being in a race chair and I ended up having my shoulders strapped up for most of the Games. It meant you started to make choices. Could you be bothered to eat when getting to the food tent was so hard? A lot of the time the answer was no. So we survived on bread and cereal and a bit of pasta from a pizza place outside the village.

All these things added up and meant there wasn't a great team spirit. Four years earlier we'd had John Anderson from the *Gladiators* television show as team manager. The thing he was very good at was motivating the team. As a personal coach you either liked him or hated him, there was nothing in between. He could be quite obnoxious and brusque but he would support any athlete on the team and he fostered a great spirit by holding team meetings every night. They weren't compulsory but you would go along and hear about how someone had got a personal best and someone else had done well in this event. It was nice to know what was happening and it was good for morale. He'd left halfway through Barcelona for reasons that never became clear and, by Atlanta, he'd been replaced by a very able administrator but someone who didn't have the same dynamic quality.

We didn't have the same camaraderie and people weren't up

for it as they had been at Barcelona because everything was such hard work. To go for a light training session ended up being a five-hour round trip because the track was so far away. The village was disgusting and there were no timetables, so nobody knew when they were meant to be competing. The preparation hadn't been good either. Atlanta highlighted the need to look at how athletes are treated before, during and after Games to get the best out of them. I am conscious that I sound bitter and twisted about this, but so many athletes were screwed up before they even got to Atlanta that there was no way they were going to compete well. They just went there with no self-confidence and feeling they had been run into the ground. They were psychologically destroyed.

To make things worse for me, Ian was very unhappy in Atlanta. I was in the apartment next to him and he and Chris Hallam were sharing with three LD athletes. Ian's view on the subject of LD participation was widely known, so it was a pretty tactless arrangement. Ian was so annoyed he went to see the manager responsible for arranging the accommodation. He said, 'You're either incompetent or malicious. Which is it?'

The manager spluttered, 'I'm incompetent.'

Ian couldn't believe that this guy had said that without even trying to defend himself. He had no balls at all.

It was a shame there was so much hassle because Ian had been pushing exceptionally well in the lead-up to Atlanta. But by the time he had got there and been through all this unnecessary grief, he was stressed out. He was also worried about my performance because, just prior to Atlanta, one of the American girls, Leanne Shannon, had been reclassified. She had been racing as a T4 athlete for a number of years but was now reclassified as a T3. There was no doubt she was borderline and I couldn't say, hand on heart, whether she was in the right class. But there was very little support from the British team officials in protesting against the classification. There is a system in place by which you can put in a protest before the start of the Games, asking the classifiers to have another look at the evidence. It happens a lot, but the attitude of the British staff was, 'It's tough, get on with it.'

I said, 'No, if we're playing to the rules then we should play to the rules.' But my protests fell on deaf ears.

My first race was the 100 metres. I was fairly stressed too with all the problems, with being away from home and with Ian not feeling very good. That's the thing that has a bigger effect on me than anything. Luckily, when it comes down to racing I am able to switch off and forget about everything else. It made no difference in that race, though. Leanne went off very quickly and won. I had to settle for second place. The moment I got off the track, some team official came up to me in the international zone and said, 'Don't worry, you're still number one in my eyes.' I thought, thanks, but I don't need that. Stuff like that doesn't help. People don't really think about what they are saying. And I got the feeling some people in Atlanta were happy that I didn't perform. I was getting a lot of media attention and it didn't suit everyone. One guy said to me, 'Bad luck,' but he had a huge grin on his face at the time. I wasn't exactly seen as a trouble-maker but I know some people didn't appreciate me being vocal about problems within the team, although I never complained outside the team environment.

I felt down but not desperate to lose the 100 metres. Before Leanne had been reclassified I felt I could win four golds but, once I knew she was racing as a T3, the best I could hope for was one or two. I had raced okay, but she was significantly better than me where the start was crucial. I'd not expected to win, so I quickly put it behind me and I also had the 800 metres later that day to focus on. I knew I could do better in that.

I didn't have a problem with Leanne personally. She was only thirteen in Atlanta and was an incredibly talented athlete. She had started racing when she was three and had won everything at the American trials, beating established people including Jean Driscoll who'd won the Boston Marathon eight times. Wheel-chair racing is so much about technique and there is no doubt Leanne had a brilliant one. She was also very strong for her age. Mary Decker, the runner, had been number one in America when she was thirteen but hadn't been able to compete in the Olympics because she was too young. Leanne's mum, who was a very pushy lady, made sure that didn't happen to her and got the Paralympic rules changed so she could compete.

A lot of the American team didn't relate to Leanne too well, but she was a phenomenon. She was beating everybody out of sight and a lot of people were dubious about her classification. A few of the T4 girls came up to me and said she should be racing with them, but I was powerless to do anything about it. One of the comments I got from the team management was, 'Don't worry, she won't be at Sydney because she'll have grown and be slower in four years' time.' It was better that people didn't say anything to me rather than coming out with stupid comments like she'll be too fat for Sydney. That sort of thing didn't help me at all.

I got my revenge in the 800 metres. I knew I needed a superb start to get anywhere and I managed it. Some people thought I'd just let Leanne go and settle for second place, but I decided I'd go with her. I sat behind her for 600 metres and edged past her coming off the last bend with 120 metres to go. I beat her by a chair length. It was a huge high crossing the finishing line first and a very different feeling from winning the gold in Barcelona when Ann had been disqualified.

My races came thick and fast and there was very little time to see Sian and Dad. As usual, Mum didn't come to see me race. She gets too nervous. She has never been to watch me, preferring to stay at home and wait for the phone calls. She has a lot of videos and watches them afterwards, but she has never been out to the Olympics or Paralympics because she would be a nervous wreck.

Next up in Atlanta were the 200 metres semi-finals. Leanne went in the first one and she pushed really well and ended up breaking the world record. We'd been taken out on to the track so we could see them race and I watched her cross the line and the big flashy announcement come up on the board. I didn't feel envious. Instead, I had that strange calm that comes every now and again. I was very relaxed and focused as I watched her go round the track on her lap of honour.

When she had finished it was my turn. I had lane seven, which is not a favourite because it's too far out, but I went out fast. I won the heat and it was a new world record, beating the one Leanne had just set. That felt great but she beat me in the final which took the gloss off it. It wasn't a great race. Both of us went slower and the feeling of anticlimax was intense.

I had a day's gap and then it was the 400 metres. It was one race after the other, with very little time between heats and final. It was a bit of a blur and all I remember about the 400 metres is that it tipped it down and I got soaked. It was my second fastest time but I lost to Leanne again. After that race I felt probably the worst I've ever felt. I'd done my absolute best and it hadn't been good enough. Then I had to come off the track and face all these people who were pitying me. It was awful. I don't say too much to other athletes and maybe they think I'm quite arrogant and a bit snooty because of it. But there is nothing you can say to make losing better, so I say nothing. It's different if it's someone I know very well. Then I'll say something but I pick my words very carefully. When I came off after the 400 metres at Atlanta, Ian was there and he just looked at me. He knew there was nothing to say.

I finished off with the marathon. I'd regretted not doing it in Barcelona, so I decided I'd enter this time. I soon wished I hadn't. It was a very hard course with lots of hills and they killed me. I was way off the leading pack and remember seeing Chantal Peticlerc at about the 10 kilometre mark, having decided that it wasn't her day, watching from the side of the road with a wry smile on her face. From 35 kilometres I felt like I was dying. In the end I got dragged along by a Swiss athlete called Andrea. I was hurting so much and every push was agony. To make matters worse, the organisers had decided to run other track events while the marathon was going on. That caused chaos as it meant the athletes in the stadium were trying to do their races in between the marathon runners coming in. Andrea and I went over the finish line together very slowly.

'Why didn't you try to sprint past me?' she asked.

'You've pulled me along for the last seven kilometres,' I said. 'It wouldn't have been fair.' She had encouraged me and was great, but I didn't want to be in Atlanta any more. I'd had enough of a horrible Games.

I came away from America with mixed feelings. I'd performed well in terms of times but not in the context of Leanne. She was the undisputed star of the games, but the team officials were proved right when they said she wouldn't be at Sydney in 2000.

By the time we got to Australia I hadn't seen her for two years because she hadn't been competing at the same level. She had got too big physically. It's the same thing that happens to some gymnasts. Now she wants to join NASA and be the first disabled person in space. Good luck to her.

I was meant to be on the afternoon flight home from Atlanta and couldn't wait to get away. The Paralympics had been a trying experience for everyone and I just wanted to be with my family and spend some time with Ian away from the Games environment. To round things off the BPA insisted I went on the media flight that night with all the other people who had done well. Reluctantly, I agreed, but I didn't enjoy it. When we got back to Heathrow it was a complete disaster getting off the plane. By the time I got into the airport all the press and television people had gone. Someone from the BPA said, 'Oh, we forgot about you.' I didn't have a problem with not being interviewed, but they had changed my flight and taken me off the plane with all the people I cared about and then forgot I was even there. That was annoying. Then, instead of passing through as a team, everybody just went their own way. It was a huge anticlimax, going through customs alone in my GB tracksuit. It was a fitting end to a Paralympics to forget.

I've never publicly slagged the BPA off because that is not positive and I always try to do the right thing and be available for them as much as I can. They by and large do a good job and have improved the quality of their service to the athletes measurably in the last few years. But sometimes I wonder why I bother. I was told very specifically as I got off the plane from Sydney, 'Leave everything, we need you to do the interviews.' I thought, you need me now, but it wasn't like that after Atlanta. I find it very frustrating. I try to be measured about it and could be a lot more cynical. It's why I keep a fairly small group of people around me and ignore everybody else.

The aftermath of Atlanta taught me to take what people say with a pinch of salt. I'd won a gold and three silvers, but that was not enough for some people. One of the British media team said to me, 'You're finished now. You should retire.' A lot of coaches told me I'd failed. If it had been coming from people I cared about, I might have been more bothered about it, but it was only upsetting for a short period. I was dropped from a lot of the team publicity, but I learnt very quickly to deal with it. It gave me a chance to get away from the negative politics for a while. Some athletes didn't deal with it so well. I know one who came very close to having a nervous breakdown from being surrounded by people telling him he hadn't done well enough. It comes down to not knowing how to manage people. Athletes are so difficult. You deliver or you don't. If I'd listened to some people after Atlanta, I'd never have continued competing and then they would have been upset because they'd have been further down the medals table in Sydney.

I'm quite bloody-minded at times and thought I'd carry on. I was only twenty-seven and I wasn't competing for the greater glorification of the British team anyway. Rightly or wrongly, I was doing it for me. Athletes compete as individuals all the time, but then, come Paralympics time, we are suddenly a team and have to deliver a predetermined number of medals. It doesn't necessarily matter where the medals come from as long as we hit the target. It's difficult for me because I don't always feel part of the team. When I go out road training, I don't think I'm doing my bit to contribute to the British team medal total. I'm thinking this is to help me perform well at London or wherever. When I've got my sporting head on I'm probably fairly arrogant, but when I'm away from it, I'm more caring. If someone has a poor performance it doesn't affect me while I'm competing, but I might worry about them afterwards. Ian says I can't change the world but I can try.

When I came home from Atlanta I remember thinking do I really want to go through all that again? Ian wasn't very happy either. He was disappointed in his own performance and because all the extra stuff that had been going on had got to him. That feeling didn't last long, though I reasoned that we only had to deal with all the extra stuff once very four years. I learnt a lot from Atlanta. It taught me to be more selfish and not let anything get in my way.

The LD issue is still trundling on today. Since Sydney it has been proved that some of the LD athletes have been cheating and what we were saying about the classification system has proved to be true. The definition of learning difficulty varies from country to country. They have tried to make it more stringent by bringing in IQ tests but if you come from a country with a lot of special deprivation and you haven't been to school, it would be hard to get through the tests. It may not mean you have a learning difficulty. All we were saying before Atlanta was that they needed to be more organised.

After Atlanta I wanted to be less involved in the political side of the sport. As the chairman of the Wheelchair Racing Association I'd been involved in selection for Atlanta and it had not been a pleasant experience. There was a selection committee and we went through the list of athletes and said who we thought should and shouldn't be in the team. It meant making some tough choices and one athlete who didn't make it took it very badly. She went to the papers. She had posted a time under the qualifying mark but, at the end of the day, the athletes were ranked on their probability of winning a medal and what they had done in the last year. We only had twelve places in the team and this athlete was seventeenth on the list. In all, twenty-five athletes posted times under the qualifying mark. It wasn't even marginal. When she put in a protest, the other people on the committee pointed the finger at me. They said it was all my doing and because this athlete was a wheelchair racer, my department, I took the rap. We'd agreed beforehand that if there was any media hassle, we'd all stick together, but everyone turned on me. I think the other people found it so much easier to blame me rather than accept collective responsibility. The problem was that someone had told the athletes that if they got what we call an A qualifying time, they would be on the plane. But when it came to selection we had twice as many people with A times as there were places.

Despite my feelings at the time, I ended up going for an interview at British Athletics a couple of weeks after I got back. I'd applied for a job as a disability development officer while I was in America. I'd decided that you can't bitch about something if you're not prepared to try to change it. I sat down and composed a hand-written application from Pensacola and then set out to find a fax machine. That proved easier said than done. Bollo and I drove all over and eventually found one ten minutes before the deadline for applications. The woman in the shop had no concept of how to make a foreign call, but the letter went off in the nick of time and I didn't think any more of it.

To my surprise I got an interview and so I went along to the offices in Birmingham. Mum drove up with me because I was still feeling jet-lagged and was sleeping sixteen hours a day. The interview panel was made up of five people, including Malcolm Arnold, the head of coaching and development, Colin Raines, of cerebral palsy sport, and Mark Southam, of LD sport. I'd had minor disagreements with all of them in the past about one thing or another and when I walked into the room and saw them all sitting there, I decided I'd failed the interview already. I did my best anyway, then went home with Mum. I wasn't holding my breath. That night I was at a Sports Council dinner in Cardiff when Mum rang and said I had to ring Malcolm Arnold. I found a phone and called him.

'Hello, Tanni, we'd like to offer you the job,' he said.

'Oh,' I replied.

'What do you mean oh?'

'Well, I didn't think you were going to offer it to me.'

'Look, it's obviously a bit of a shock. Take some time to think about it.'

I talked it over with my family. Ian thought I should take the job, but Mum and Dad weren't sure. It would mean moving to Birmingham, finding a new training facility and having to balance my athletics with a full-time job. But I decided to take it. I thought it would be exciting to have a job at last and that it would be exciting to work within the governing body. I also thought the fact British Athletics had created the post showed how seriously they wanted to take disability sport. I soon found out that there was an incredible amount of work that needed doing. British Athletics just was not equipped to deal with disability sport. There wasn't the structure in place to do the job properly and the project was probably a couple of years ahead of its time.

I would say I was tolerated by some people within the governing body while I was working there. Some of the development officers were great and felt disability athletics should come under the mainstream umbrella, but I didn't get a terribly good reception from a couple of the national team coaches. That was frustrating. Coming so soon after Atlanta, the last thing I needed was more problems with authority.

Now I try to avoid harping on about Atlanta because it sounds like I am bitter and I don't mean to be. I'd never tried to stitch up any of the team management and I could have said an awful lot more when I came home. The press were interested in any story surrounding how hard Atlanta had been but I wasn't interested in that. That's not my way. If I have a problem with something I tell the people concerned. They probably think, oh God, it's her again, but life could have been a lot harder for them.

The fact is some of the management we had in Atlanta were not there to provide support for the athletes. I got to America feeling as if I'd been pulled apart by everything that was going on. I actually pushed pretty well in Atlanta and was setting personal bests and world records, but I was fed up. I came away feeling utterly desolate and disillusioned with the sport.

Chapter Eight

The Queen and I

WHEN I look back at Atlanta now, I think the one great thing about it was that the media coverage in Britain started to get better at that time. A lot of that was down to Helen Rollason who became a good friend. Helen was doing programmes for the BBC every day and she was there for all my races. When I came off after my 800 metres she was standing right by the finishing line with a camera crew. She had a huge smile on her face.

'Tanni, come here,' she said. So I went over and she gave me a big hug and a kiss. Then she said, 'Would you mind doing an interview with us?' That was Helen's way. Very polite. I mean, as if anyone was going to turn down an interview with her.

We met up at sporting events and I enjoyed seeing her. She was always very fair to me, but that doesn't mean she shirked asking hard questions. She was just very nice about the way she did it. After my 100 metres in Atlanta, she asked me why I hadn't won, but the way she phrased it meant I didn't mind. She was a really nice person to have around.

I first met her at the World Championships in Holland in 1990. I went up to her and said, 'You're Helen Rollason of *Newsround.*'

She smiled and said, 'I work for *Grandstand* now.'

I felt such a fool, but she didn't hold it against me. Helen was the first broadcaster to see the Paralympics as pure sport. She wanted to give it the best possible coverage and was hugely ambitious. She was a pioneer. Others have since taken up the baton, including Clare Balding and Paul Dickinson. The attitude at the BBC is changing and much of it is down to Helen and the regard in which she was held. She must have faced a lot of challenges to become a female sports presenter and it can't have been easy convincing people she was qualified to speak about football or host *Grandstand*. But she got her job on merit. It wasn't a token gesture. She was good and she paved the way for others, Sue Barker and Gaby Yorath, for instance.

I spoke to Helen a few times after she was diagnosed with cancer. It was so sad that it happened to such a nice person. She was going to come to our wedding, but I got a letter from her the day beforehand saying she couldn't make it because she was going back into hospital. It was a sad, lovely letter and I cried as I read it. Helen had been there for all the big things that had happened in my life and the wedding was the only one she missed. I never saw her again.

She tried to keep her illness private and I didn't realise she was as bad as she was. I'd seen her shortly before the wedding at a function and she looked fantastic.

'Have you had the invitation?' I asked.

'What invitation?'

'To my wedding.'

She was gobsmacked. 'What, you're inviting *me* to your wedding?'

'I'd really like you to come.'

She was touched and that was nice. We talked about everything except her illness, but then I said, 'God, you look really good.'

Helen filled up a bit and just shook her head. She didn't say anything and I put my head down and rambled on for a bit about something inane. She didn't want to talk about it. She just wanted to get on with things.

I vividly remember hearing that she had died. Someone from the BBC rang me up at home in Birmingham. Then I heard from someone else at the Sports Council. I listened to the news that night and cried. I didn't go to the funeral because I thought I would have been too upset and I hate funerals anyway. I don't regret not going and took part in a memorial programme soon afterwards. They came to do the filming at the British Athletics offices and we sat in the room of Dave Moorcroft, the chief executive. The presenter was a good friend of Helen's and we sat there talking about all the good times we'd had with her. When the cameras were rolling I was fine, but when they stopped we reminisced about many different events and I ended up bawling my eyes out.

Helen made a tremendous difference to women's sport and minority sport. She wasn't afraid to say what she thought and she got things done. It was such a shame that she missed out on Sydney because she would have had a blast. For the first time the Paralympics received huge coverage and she would have loved that. Seeing other crews there without her was weird. Helen would have been so satisfied to see how things had progressed from the time of Atlanta and before.

Things were progressing for me. I've been very fortunate throughout my career to be invited to participate in a lot of interesting things, from garden parties at Buckingham Palace to *A Question of Sport* on television. I appreciate that athletics has opened a lot of doors for me. I have been to Buckingham Palace on quite a few occasions and have met almost all the royal family. Mum's a staunch royalist, whereas Ian's a republican, so I usually take her with me to the royal events. Towards the end of 1993 Mum had a phone call from someone at the palace asking if I'd accept an MBE if I was offered one. I was away competing but Mum said yes and then a letter came through the post from the Prime Minister's Principal Private Secretary, Alex Allan, saying they'd decided to confer the MBE on me, did I want it and, if so, could I keep my mouth shut. If you tell anybody before the list comes out, they will not give it to you. Mum was incredibly thrilled by it all and I was excited because I was only twenty-four and that was fairly young to be getting an MBE.

I had to be vetted to make sure I was a reasonable human being and then it was off to the palace on 16 March 1994. There were hundreds of other people getting awards and it was all incredibly well organised. The worst part was having to get dressed up. I'd been off with Mum to buy a hat but I hated it. I've never worn it since. I don't like having to wear dresses and hats and the last time I met the Queen I made a point of keeping my purple Doc Martens boots on!

The ceremony took place inside a great hall. Beforehand a man, dripping with gold braid and medals, came up to me.

'You don't recognise me, do you?'

I desperately scoured my memory bank but couldn't come up with anything. 'Er, no, I'm sorry.'

'I'm Sir Richard Vickers from the Winston Churchill Memorial Trust.'

I felt so embarrassed. This man had helped pay for my trip to Australia and I couldn't even remember him. When I'd met him before I'd thought he was a nice old bloke who didn't say too much but was very polite. Now I realised his part-time job was working in the Queen's household and he had a million letters after his name. He was dressed up in all this grandeur whereas the last time I'd seen him he was wearing grey trousers and a dull cardigan. So I said, 'I didn't recognise you in your clothes.'

I regretted it almost before the words were out, but he laughed and was very charming and told me how the ceremony would work. I was given a clip to fasten on my jacket so that it was easy for the Queen to pin the medal on. There were about ten Paralympic athletes getting MBEs, including swimmers Chris Holmes and Sarah Bailey, and I remember *Morse* star John Thaw and evergreen disc jockey Jimmy Young were also there.

An aide told us that the Queen would ask us a couple of questions and when she said, 'Thank you' that was the end of the conversation. There was to be no clapping and no photography. When my turn came the Queen smiled and asked me about Barcelona and whether the team had done well. I avoided putting my foot in it this time and came out with something about how wonderful it all was. Then I nodded my head because I couldn't curtsey.

Whatever training the Queen gets, it works. She has the ability to make you feel as if you are the only person in the room. She is fantastic at it. How she remembers all the right questions to ask is amazing. There are an awful lot of people there from different fields, but there is nobody prompting her or telling her what to say. It was hugely impressive.

Afterwards I was escorted out into an ante chamber. They took the medal off me and put it in a small velvet box. There was a card inside explaining when and where I was allowed to wear it. There are only certain occasions when women are allowed to wear the MBE medal and the rest of the time they have to make do with a miniature, which you can buy from the palace for about £100. I never wore it again and keep it in a safe at the bank, along with my Paralympic medals. I've always done that with my medals. It's not that they're worth a great amount materially, but I don't want anyone breaking into the house and stealing them. Once my medals go into the safe, I rarely bother to get them out. After I won my medals in Sydney people wanted to take pictures of me with all my golds, so I went to the bank. That was the first time I'd seen them since I'd put them in. Other people might keep them in the house or frame them, but that's not for me. I think they mean different things to different people. They mean more to Mum and Dad because they are tangible reminders of what I've done. And for Mum they probably mean a bit extra because she has never been there to see me win them.

When I got my OBE in the 2000 New Years Honours list, I had to send my MBE back. You are not allowed to have both at the same time and you get a very polite letter asking if you would return it. So I sent my MBE off in the post, special delivery. I could have received the OBE at Cardiff Castle but opted to go back to Buckingham Palace. This time Prince Charles conducted the ceremony. It was exactly the same as before except, being an OBE, I was further up the pecking order.

The thing I remember most about the OBE was that Mum, Sian and I went to the Savoy Hotel afterwards for tea. That was great. It was all you could eat and I think Sian and I embarrassed Mum because we devoured several plates of sandwiches, cakes and scones.

'You can't possibly want any more,' she said.

'Oh, yes we can,' I said as we tucked into another plate.

A lot of other people from the palace had the same idea. You could tell by the hats and weird creations people were wearing. There were some truly horrendous ones, but it was great sitting in the Savoy with my OBE, people watching, and eating loads of cream cakes.

The tea tents at Buckingham Palace garden parties are incredible too. They have lavish sandwiches, gorgeous cakes and delicious ice creams. They are very civilised occasions. The grounds are lovely, as you would imagine, and you naturally try to have a wander and explore. You can walk quite a long way. One of the things I remember being impressed by was the toilets. They look like a huge shed in the gardens, but they are the most impressive public loos you could ever come across.

I have always been interested in history so being at the palace was fascinating. At one huge reception, which is only held every ten years and is like a who's who, I found myself being taken on a private tour. Because some parts of the palace are not very accessible, I was allocated my own personal footman. That was incredible because he knew the history behind every painting and every artefact.

At the first garden party Mum and I went to we were lucky enough to meet the Queen. You stand in lines and she decides who to speak to. As she walked along the line I remember feeling nervous. Then the Queen stopped and spoke to us. 'Do you watch your daughter race?' she asked Mum.

'No,' she replied. 'I get far too nervous for that.'

'Quite understandable,' said the Queen. 'Did you manage to get across the grass all right?'

'Yes, it was fine,' I answered.

I have to admit I have had a couple of embarrassing moments with royalty. The first came when the Emperor of Japan was visiting Cardiff Castle. There was a big lunch laid on and someone asked if I wanted to go in first because my seat was in the middle and so it would avoid everyone having to move. I went into the hall but stopped at the entrance and started talking to a couple of waiters by the door. It's often far more interesting talking to people who work in those places than anyone else, so we were gossiping away when the Emperor and Empress of Japan walked round the corner. The Queen was there too. Because of the angle of my chair, I was blocking the Emperor's way, but I didn't want to dart out of the way as that would have looked incredibly rude. So I ended up having a chat with him and he was absolutely lovely because he had no idea who I was. Eventually he moved on. A line of aides followed him with horror etched on their faces because I hadn't been formally introduced. I sloped away as quickly as I could.

'Brilliant,' I said to the waiters. 'I've probably just mortally offended the Emperor of Japan.'

The other time was when Buckingham Palace put on a reception for the Paralympic squad after Sydney. I was talking to two of my friends, Danny Crates and Lloyd Upsdell, in the corner of a room. We were sitting by a huge sideboard.

'What do you reckon's in there?' said Lloyd.

'I don't know,' said Danny.

'Why don't we have a look?' I suggested.

We didn't think anybody was looking, so I quietly opened a drawer and had a nose around. I remember thinking it was odd because all there was inside was a raffle ticket and a South African plug adapter. Then we heard a voice from behind us.

'Are you having a good time?'

We spun round and there was Princess Anne. I slammed the drawer shut behind me and said, 'Er yes, lovely, thanks.'

Luckily, she saw the funny side of it and she was very nice.

She had been to the Olympics so she knew what it was like and we had a long discussion about that. That was great because, in truth, the conversations you have with the royals are usually fairly superficial. Sophie Rhys-Jones, the Countess of Wessex, is probably the one I talked to for longest. We met after Sydney and she introduced herself by saying, 'Hi, I'm Sophie.' She was very approachable and down to earth. She seemed genuinely interested in Sydney and how it had changed my life, but was obviously struggling with how the media treated her. She seemed lovely but was having a hard time dealing with journalists having a go at her just because they didn't like what she was wearing that day. That must be awful. I think there is still a place for the monarchy but I also think some of the younger royals have lost their way a bit. The media has changed towards them and they haven't adapted.

I consider myself very fortunate to have been able to visit Buckingham Palace and I feel the same way about Downing Street. Those places are part of our national heritage. I've been to Downing Street a few times and have met John Major, Tony Blair and Margaret Thatcher. The building itself is like a Tardis. It looks small from the outside but once you walk through the door, it goes back a long way. The front door opens into an entrance hall with a grand staircase and there are portraits of past prime ministers decorating the walls. On one occasion Mum had come with me and we were looking at a painting on the wall. Dad loves pictures, but he was at home looking after our dog, and Mum said, 'He'd love that wouldn't he?'

Then we heard a voice saying, 'It is a beautiful painting, isn't it?'

It was John Major. He stayed with us for about fifteen minutes and explained that some pictures were on loan and that he could choose a certain number of them himself. He was very charming and open and spoke to us about life as prime minister. I asked him if he liked doing these receptions and he smiled and said most of them were okay. He was not affected at all by his position and was very easy to talk to. I take people at face value and he seemed a nice, genuine guy.

Although I did politics at university, I have to admit I do get switched off by party politics. I don't like the way they just bicker at each other and there's never anything that's completely positive. Whatever anybody does, there is always someone else diving in and having a go. It's pretty childish and I started to get tired of it towards the end of the Tory government. I thought John Major was a decent man but probably not the right person for that job. I don't think a lot of people ever forgave him for getting rid of Thatcher. I thought the Tories ended up losing the plot. I'm not a socialist but I'm probably more comfortable with New Labour than with the Tories because I find all the race issues and the 'I'm all right Jack' attitude a bit unsettling. My politics changed when I moved to Birmingham. I'd come from a fairly affluent part of Cardiff and when you grow up in that sheltered environment, you tend to think everyone lives like that. But when I came to Birmingham I realised there were a lot of people who really didn't have anything at all. It opened my eyes and made me appreciate how some people struggle financially.

Including local elections, I have voted Tory, Labour, Lib Dem, Green and Monster Raving Loony Party. The latter was in local elections in Birmingham. I didn't like any of the candidates but felt I should vote. So I went for the Loonies. I suppose it was my protest vote. More recently, with my profile high again after

Sydney, people have tried to get me involved in politics. I met Alastair Campbell at the finishing line of the London Marathon and he asked me what I was going to vote in the general election. I told him Labour and he asked if I would help at all with the general election campaign. Mum's a Tory and was horrified but I decided I would get involved in a small way and so I was featured in a party political broadcast. They spent a day filming and I was on for about two seconds, but I got a huge bouquet of flowers from Tony Blair as a result.

As someone who is proud to be Welsh, I often get asked about my thoughts on devolution. My view is I don't agree with devolution for Wales unless England has its own parliament as well. If England had had its own representative assembly, or whatever you want to call it, I'd have voted yes. As it was, I voted no. I think they should have learnt from the Sports Council. For years they had a Great Britain Sports Council. Then, for whatever reason, they decided to split them up and it just didn't work. It's the same with devolution. The only change most people in Cardiff have seen from there being a Welsh Assembly is house prices have gone up.

I get frustrated with politics but am interested in it and, after Sydney, I was asked to go on *Question Time*, the political panel show on BBC1. They like having a 'normal' person on the panel because they feel it makes the politicians more honest. I always try to do things if I am asked, and I thought it would be interesting, so I went along to the studios in Manchester. They sit all the panellists in a room together for about half an hour before the start. A couple of the others had their spin doctors with them. I had Sian. Martin Bell was on the programme that night and he was very sweet to me. 'This is the most terrifying thing I've ever done in my life,' he said. 'I don't know why I'm back.'

Someone else said, 'Don't worry, it's not that bad.' Nobody was very convinced and they all started joking about how terrible it really was. They quickly ended up admitting it was horrific.

Another panellist said to me, 'Don't worry if you don't know anything about politics.' I don't think he meant to be patronising but I told him I was a politics graduate. Then I said, 'It's okay for me because I'm an athlete. I can be a total fruit loop and they'll just say she's an athlete who doesn't know much. It's not like you guys. It's your careers.'

As soon as I'd said that, I wished I hadn't. They were all very nervous and that probably didn't help. One guy's hands were shaking so hard that he had to clasp them together. 'You seem very calm,' one of them said to me and I was. It was funny because I felt the same as I do at the start of a race but without the throwing up. After I have been sick before a race and I'm in the final call room where they keep the athletes before going on the track, I often feel very relaxed. I began to focus and the adrenaline began to pump. 'This is what I do,' I said. 'I'm used to pressure situations.'

You don't get to see the questions but you have a good idea of what's going to come up from the current news. The fact Lord Faulkner was on meant there was going to be some stuff about the Dome, and race was the big issue of that week. They had a warm-up question about whether it was right that women should fight on the front line. The journalist Simon Heffer said how horrific it was and how women being killed on the front line would drive men to distraction. I was on next and said I'd have thought the sight of anyone being killed would be horrific, whether they were male or female. I also said we should spend more time trying not to start wars in the first place and that warfare has changed so much that there wasn't a front line anyway. You do all the fighting from your nuclear bunker. That got me going and I enjoyed it after that. Being the non-political panellist I was also lucky because David Dimbleby went easy on me, whereas he gave some of the others a grilling.

By the time I did *Question Time* I was fairly used to appearing on television and the radio. I like it and feel comfortable in front of microphones and cameras, but it wasn't always like that. When I started presenting a programme called *Sport First* on BBC Radio, about sport for people with disabilities, I was very nervous and there were a few occasions when I thought I needed a sick bucket in the studio.

I think the thing that made me realise I had finally arrived as an athlete was when I was asked to appear on *A Question of Sport* for the first time. When I was growing up the programme was huge and everybody would watch it. I was the first Paralympian to be asked on so that was an honour. The only trouble being my sporting knowledge is awful. Because I spend a lot of time away from home I don't get to see a lot through the summer months and, although I'd watched a fair bit of rugby, I've always preferred individual sports rather than team ones. I can relate to them better and I like the excitement that comes from it being one person against everyone else. Cycling, gymnastics and triathlon are my favourites. Cycling is interesting because it's the closest sport to what we do as wheelchair athletes. I feel closer to it than I do to athletics. I also watch speed-skating because that is similar too. There was talk of me actually competing at the Winter Olympics in 1994. Some of the Japanese wheelchair racers double up and do skating, so it was suggested I could spend six months learning the skills involved and then go to Lillehammer in Norway. But I thought I'd need two years' training and I didn't think it would have been right to go. It would have devalued what I do. Apart from those things, however, my knowledge of mainstream sport is pretty poor. Not surprisingly, our team on *A Question of Sport* got thrashed.

Funnily enough, I was a lot more nervous about *A Question of Sport* than *Question Time*, but Ian Botham helped me relax when we had a lunch beforehand. He was good fun and put me at ease. It was 1993 and being on the programme gave me wider public recognition than actually winning four gold medals in Barcelona the previous year. For me it was the icing on the cake after Spain.

Since then I have done lots of television work. One of the funniest things was when I was double-booked to do *Through The Keyhole* and *Heaven and Earth* on the same day. I had two film crews in my house in Birmingham bickering about who should go first. In the end the *Through The Keyhole* team started filming while Alice Beer, the presenter of *Heaven and Earth*, sat in the kitchen doing her Lloyd Grossman impersonation. She was a great laugh. The range of shows I do has got a lot wider. In 2001 I did *They Think It's All Over*. I suppose it's an adult version of *A Question of Sport* and I was a bit nervous about how they would treat me. It was most memorable for Chris Eubank. He tried to take over the show at one point but the other panellists were incredibly rude to him. Jonathan Ross said something along the lines of, 'Why don't you just sod off home?' The language was a lot stronger, though. I felt sorry for him because the others ganged up on him. He was getting a lot of unnecessary stick. At one point Jonathan Ross said to me, 'Are you okay?' I said, 'I'm fine, but it's not my thing to abuse people like that.' It was all so scripted and pre-planned.

Being on *A Question of Sport* for the first time was probably the high point on my television appearances. When I was asked to go back on the show in 1997, I was really surprised. It was the year after the Paralympics in Atlanta so I wasn't in the public eye. This time it was being filmed in Manchester and Mum and Sian came to watch. I was on Ally McCoist's team and he seemed a nice guy. To my surprise we won. And then I heard the audience gasp. All these heads turned and from the corner of the stage I saw Michael Aspel. He wandered over to the set and stood in between the two teams, holding that famous red book. I thought they were going to get John Parrott and thought poor sod. Then he said, 'Tanni Grey, this is your life.' I turned to Ally and he had a massive grin on his face. Then Michael Aspel put a microphone in my face and said, 'Would you like to say anything?'

I was absolutely shocked and said, 'No.' People usually come out with something very witty or pithy, but I just sat there with my mouth open, looking completely vacant. I think Michael Aspel was getting worried. He had a look on his face that said please say something. The only thing I could think to say was that I had nothing smarter to wear than a pair of jeans.

I looked up into the audience and saw Mum and Sian killing themselves. I thought, my God, they knew all along. My main worry was that I had nothing to wear. I was rushed off set and taken to a dressing room. Ian had brought some clothes for me to put on, but they were not the best. So I went on *This Is Your Life* wearing blue shoes, a green and white skirt, brown tights, a green blouse and a blue jacket. Thanks, Ian.

Things suddenly began to make sense. When I'd been in the make-up room for *A Question of Sport*, they had been very stroppy when I tried to go outside. At one point I was physically dragged back in by the make-up girl.

'The producers don't like the audience to know who's going to be on,' she said.

'I was only trying to find my family,' I replied.

I thought her reaction was a bit over the top but didn't think any more of it. What I didn't know was all my friends and family were walking past the door to get to the *This Is Your Life* set. Afterwards I also recalled that there had been signs all over the place for some game show. But there wasn't a game show at all. That was the code for *This Is Your Life*.

I have to admit there were quite a few people whom I hoped hadn't been invited. I imagine everyone who gets on to the show thinks like that.

'Who've you got?' I asked an assistant.

'I can't say, but you'll have a great time,' she said.

I wasn't convinced. 'I don't care if I'm going to have a good time, who've you got?'

When I went out Ian was already sitting there. It was all a blur. Sian came on and said something, which meant a lot because she hates things like that, and some friends, who hadn't been asked to be on the set, had come along to be in the audience which was lovely. Then the guests started being introduced by Michael Aspel. Ingrid Lauridsen had come over which was great and Sue Roberts, my childhood friend, was there. Then came the finale. They always bring someone out who you haven't seen for years or who has flown thousands of miles and I began to get nervous. They showed clips from Atlanta and were building up the rivalry between me and Leanne Shannon. I thought, oh no, they haven't got Leanne. We got on all right but I always thought Leanne's mother was a bit of a nightmare. I said to myself, just smile and say thanks for coming. If you look at the film I have a plastic smile on my face at that point. And then they brought on Jenni, my coach, and the relief was huge. I couldn't believe she'd come all the way from Australia. We had a tremendous party at the studios which was the best I've ever been to. All my friends were there and I just couldn't believe they had managed to keep it a secret.

If I'd had the choice, I have to admit that I probably wouldn't have done *This Is Your Life*. I don't really like that kind of public exposure where they go through your life in half an hour. I watch it because I'm as nosy as the next person. When the producers got in touch, Mum and Dad discussed whether I'd want to do it. Ian said he thought I probably wouldn't want to, but Mum, Dad and Sian decided it would be a good time to be on. They knew how down I'd been after Atlanta and felt it was quite important for me to do it. If nothing else it would help recover my public profile and I think it was one in the eye for all those people who told me I'd been such a failure after Atlanta.

Chapter Nine

High Achiever

FOR ME disability has not been about overcoming things. That is why I find it hard to understand when people say I'm a role model. I'm just an athlete who happens to have a disability. If people do see me as an inspiration I'd hope that it is because I'm good at what I do, not because I'm supposedly 'brave and wonderful'.

You cannot forget about your disability because it is there all the time in your daily life. But I don't think I've had to deal with any great obstacles because I'm in a wheelchair. At the same time I am aware that some people might not have dealt with their disabilities as well and they might take some encouragement from what I've done. If they do, that's great and I suppose that is an achievement.

I remember as a kid being inspired by watching the London Marathon on television. Now I realise there might be some kids who are watching me and feeling the same way. Shortly after I did a race in Balmoral, which was shown on television, I had a call from Karen Lewis, who works at Scottish Disability Sport. 'Guess what?' she said. 'We've had a stack of kids ringing us saying they want to know how they can start wheelchair racing. You'd never believe the interest.' That is really nice. It's something tangible that I can be proud of.

I also get quite a lot of letters. I had one from a woman who saw me on a television show with Gloria Hunniford. She didn't know who I was but had heard me talking about spina bifida. She was pregnant and had been told that she was going to have a spina bifida baby. She'd already decided to keep the baby but wrote to say that I'd helped convince her that she had made the right decision. I got the letter about a week before she was due to give birth and I wrote back and told her to contact me whenever she wanted. Some time afterwards I received a long, seven-page letter from her all about Harry. He'd had a chest infection and bladder and kidney failure and I remember saying to Ian, 'Oh God, something awful's happened to Harry.' I flicked straight to the end of the letter and was so relieved to find he was okay. She'd spent an awful lot of time writing to me just to say thanks and that she knew that, if Harry was going to have to be in a wheelchair, it would be okay.

That's why it's good for me to do things like *Question Time*. You don't get asked on those sort of programmes just because people feel sorry for you. It helps show disabled people as normal human beings. And now, more and more, the reports about me focus on my athletics. People always used to say to me, 'What's wrong with you?' I absolutely hate that question because there's nothing wrong with me. The next time someone asks me that I'm going to say, 'I've got three heads actually.' The other thing people say is, 'What's it like being confined to a wheelchair?' I don't know because I'm not confined to anything. I do get out of the chair. I do sleep and have a bath. There was a bit about me on Trevor McDonald's programme recently and they interviewed Steve Redgrave. He said it was amazing what I'd achieved because I'd had to overcome so much. It was very sweet of him to say that but it wasn't true. I haven't overcome anything any other athlete hasn't had to.

Now I think I am being accepted purely as an athlete, rather than a victim who has fought against the odds. If that inspires people, then great. I get lots of letters from people asking for my autograph which is nice and I keep in touch with one class at a primary school in Germany. They started writing to me after the 1993 Berlin Marathon because they saw me on television. They used to have two girls in their class who were in wheelchairs. We've kept in contact and I sent them a postcard from Sydney. I get the odd letter addressed to Tanni Grey, Athlete, Redcar. They still find their way to my house, which is good for the ego.

Martin, who hates being called my agent but takes care of that side of things, says I need to see myself differently, but I try to keep my feet on the ground. Being an athlete is a fragile thing and you never know when it's going to end. All you know is that it will end at some point and if you get too excited about it now, you might find it hard to deal with when you do finish. I am lucky to have an agent like Martin. Although he wants me to make money, he will not make me do things that he doesn't feel are right. He started working with me in 1997. I was with an agency before that, but I wasn't too happy with them. Martin, who'd met me briefly before at a function, was setting up on his own. He asked to meet and after a cup of coffee I decided to work with him.

He takes care of the things I am not comfortable with, like asking for money. I also hate saying no to people. Martin's better at that and it means I don't do too much.

I joke he's my agent but he thinks he's different from the normal sports agent. I bought him a sheepskin coat as a joke, because that's what they all wear, but he's never touched it.

The London Marathon winners' podium, 1996.
Liz McColgan is behind me.

Seconds before breaking the world record in
the 200m semi-finals – Atlanta, 1996.

Back to local racing in Cardiff after the Atlanta Games, alongside Ian (*far left*) and fellow Welsh
athlete Richard Powell.

Leanne Shannon celebrates winning gold for the USA in the 100m – Atlanta, 1996.

Interviewing in Atlanta with Helen Rollason – a great supporter of the Paralympic movement.

I broke the world record in the semis – but only got a silver in the 200m final in Atlanta.

Approaching the start of the 800m demonstration event during the main Olympic Games – Atlanta, 1996.

Tanni Grey – This Is Your Life!

Being presented with the famous red book in 1997.

Working on the BT Athletics development programme.

Training on my wedding day.

Winning my first European title in the 800m in Budapest, 1998.

Arriving at the church with my dad, Peter.

A kiss for the camera? Not a chance! *Hello!* magazine covered our wedding.

'an and I cut the cake, which was made by Mum.

A high-altitude honeymoon!

Ian racing in Switzerland - May, 1998.

He's been a big help, though, especially since Sydney when I have been inundated with requests for all manner of things.

For me, Sydney 2000 is already an eternity ago. It has gone. But people still remember it as if it was yesterday and I have been surprised at how much recognition I have had since then. It is mainly me who is getting on to the television shows but that's only because I've been around longer. When I stop, things will not go back to the way they were because the Paralympics is about more than one person. But I'd like to think I've helped change attitudes to disability sport in the long term and maybe I've changed the parameters. After the Paralympics it wasn't just the London cabbies who said, 'You're the girl from Sydney.' I was in first class in a train shortly afterwards and three blokes in suits said, 'You're the girl off the TV.' All that helps and shows there is wider appreciation than there used to be.

Martin and Ian see it more than I do. Martin is always saying I have to look at the bigger picture. But I just see myself as an athlete, not a role model or an inspiration, and you can't say I've changed the face of the Paralympics because I haven't.

When I took my job with British Athletics in Birmingham I was determined to be treated equally. The development office was based on the first floor so I'd go in and drag my chair up and down the stairs after me. That caused some awkwardness because people didn't know how to react to seeing me crawling around on the floor, but I was determined to work upstairs with the others. I started getting to work before everybody else so they would be spared seeing me wandering around on my hands and knees. Some people didn't know whether to help me or not. There were also certain people I did not want to feel beholden to and I didn't want them to be able to use the fact they carried my chair for me against me in the future. I made good friends with Jo Tranter, who worked in the same department, and she would carry my bag for me. She was very laid-back about it, but there were others whom I didn't want to provide with any excuse. The staircase was wide enough for other people to get by me as I was bouncing down the stairs, but the development office was moved to the ground floor fairly soon after I started. Dave Moorcroft, the head of British Athletics, understood exactly why I was insistent on working upstairs, but I don't think he was happy with me crawling all over the place, and I prefer not to embarrass people unnecessarily.

I settled in Birmingham very quickly. I had some nice neighbours and Ian's sister, Faith, lived just around the corner. We'd met a few years before at Ian's graduation and got on really well. It was the right time for me to leave home, but I didn't want to go all the way to Redcar to be with Ian because that would have felt as if I was being pulled away. If I could, I would move back to Cardiff like a shot because I love it there, but I liked being in Birmingham. It gave me a new perspective on life.

I'd come home from Atlanta not knowing what I wanted to do with my life. I was seriously thinking about walking away from representing the British squad and just competing on my own in marathons and at major events like the Swiss Nationals. But things eventually calmed down. I realised that I wasn't that special and that Atlanta had been hard for a lot of people. Afterwards everyone said we can't have another Paralympics like that. Coaches, athletes and people from disability groups started talking to each other in a way they hadn't done before. Nobody could forget the past but people genuinely wanted to make it better.

Having a full-time job gave me something different to think

about too. On my first day I had to go to Lilleshall to give a presentation on my job to the national coaches and development officers. As I knew practically nothing about the job at that point, this was quite hard, but I received great support from two of the coaches, while I think the other eight saw it as an interesting challenge. The development officers, Angela Little-wood, John Temperton and Bob Allen, were fantastic. They saw the inclusion of disabled athletes within the main governing body as a natural step.

It was hard work. I was in charge of seventeen regions, and in some of those we were trying to generate athletes out of nothing. The problem was we were using the swimming model and trying to plant that on disability athletics and it didn't work. Whatever discipline you do in swimming, you are all in a pool and doing basically the same things. In athletics, training and requirements vary much more; a field eventer and sprinter will need totally different things. Swimming also had a local develop-ment network to start with and we didn't. The idea behind the project, getting us integrated into mainstream athletics, was sound, but the reality proved much more difficult.

Things went from bad to worse in 1997 when British Athletics called in the administrators. I'd just moved away from home and had got a mortgage so I was worried like everybody else. The funding for my job came from British Telecom sponsorship, so I knew I was probably safer than most, but it was still a difficult period. There had been rumours that athletics had no money and Dave Moorcroft had been brought in to take the problem by the scruff of the neck. One day he called us all in and we knew it was bad news.

'Due to financial difficulties we cannot go on operating like this,' he said.

'What's going to happen to our jobs,' someone asked.

'I honestly don't know,' he said.

In the end some jobs went. Athletics had enjoyed years of having lots of money but hadn't looked after it very well. Those losing their jobs were the innocent victims of that. I think it was a very brave thing for Dave Moorcroft to do. It must have been horrific to come in in the morning and have to make people redundant, but he is an honest man who is passionate about his sport and he was not going to do anything unethical.

The funny thing was that my job contract went to LD Sport in the shake-up. After all I had said about LD Sport in the run-up in Atlanta, there was a certain irony about that.

'Well who would have thought it?' said Mark Southam, who worked at LD Sport, when I met him.

'I know, I know,' I said.

To be fair to Mark, he completely understood that I had a very different point of view and he didn't give me any grief at all.

Having the job meant my days had a lot more structure. I didn't want to train on the roads in the morning because they were so busy, so I'd do some weights before going to work, put in some miles during my dinner break and then have a session in the evening. Faith used to cook me a lot of meals and the local people were really supportive when they saw me out on the roads, but there wasn't much time for a social life. Fridays would be taken up with travelling to see Ian or waiting for him to arrive, Sundays were competition days and that meant you'd probably have an early night on Saturday.

I was soon back in the swing of competing and managed to put Atlanta behind me. In 1997 I went to Athens for the demonstration race at the mainstream World Championships and came third. Louise Sauvage won and Chantal Peticlerc came second but it wasn't a great race. We were all quite strung out and that meant it was not very exciting for those watching. Athens was also a difficult place to get around in a wheelchair and I remember coughing up lots of black stuff because of the smog. The British hotel wasn't accessible so I stayed with the Australian team as I knew quite a few of them from training in Perth. Going to different countries makes you realise that disabled people are treated differently around the world. Some countries treat them badly and there are widely varying opinions on access. In Spain they will say they have great access and you'll find it means they have ramps with 1 in 2 inclines that you need a pickaxe to get up.

The following year the World Wheelchair Games were held in Birmingham. That was strange. It can be hard to get too excited about major championships when they are held at home. Racing on the track you spend day after day training on means it doesn't feel the same somehow. The Games had a very low profile and nobody came to watch. That was a shame because Birmingham completely redid the Alexandra Stadium and spent a lot of money, but I don't think there was a market for a disability world championships in this country at that time.

Being in Britain the competition ran on time, but there were problems. I stayed in the university because I don't think you can get into competition mode if you are living at home. You have to be part of the environment to get geared up. For some strange reason, I was put on the floor with the Tunisian male athletes. There were only curtains on the doors of the showers and the toilets, and some of the Tunisians felt it was highly amusing to keep whipping them open. It was just very annoying.

After one day I'd had enough so I went to see the team manager.

'I don't want to stay there, so can I move?' I said.

'I'm not sure whether there's any space available anywhere else,' he said.

'Well if I don't move, I'm going home.'

That conversation was overheard by Peter Arnott, who worked with a lot of the amputee squad. He had caused a bit of tension within the team because he had pushed very hard to make sure that his squad was based together on the same floor. It was seen as quite élitist that he had managed to bypass the system to get his way, but he is a very strong-willed individual and gets things done.

'You can come and stay with us if you want?' he said.

'That's great,' I said.

Others were not so sure. 'You want to be careful about moving to that floor,' someone warned me. Some people didn't agree with Peter's ideas. My view was that he looked after his athletes superbly and would do anything for them, and that I would be 'safe' on this floor. We don't agree on everything but if I was at a major games and wanted something done, Peter's the man I'd go to.

Before I knew it four or five blokes from his squad were in my room moving my stuff upstairs. It was much better. There was a system for taking showers and using the loos which got rid of the embarrassment of walking in on someone. Peter also made sure there was plan in case there was a fire. We were in a tower block and there were loads of wheelchair-users, but there wasn't a recognised system for what would happen if it caught fire. Peter sorted that out. If one of his athletes hadn't piggybacked me out of there, he would have killed them.

I had some great fun with the guys. One night before the

competition started, I was going into the building when all Peter's guys came running down the stairs. They were screaming and laughing.

'What's going on?' I yelled at one athlete. He grabbed me by the arm and yanked me round the corner and we all tore out of the building at a rate of knots.

'There,' he said. 'What do you think?'

I looked at the side of the building and couldn't believe my eyes. They had draped an enormous Union Jack down the side of this huge tower block by threading it through the windows. It was so big you could see it from the other end of the university campus. Then we all stood there, in the twilight, singing the national anthem. It was as emotional as actually winning a medal. All these foreign athletes must have been wondering what was going on, but it didn't go down well with the team management. 'We don't do that sort of thing,' I was told. The truth is things like that make it fun and build team spirit, but there were quite a few killjoys in athletics.

It was the same in Sydney. We were living at the bottom of a hill and had to pick up our duvets from the top. There was a strong wind blowing and after I'd got mine, I suddenly had an idea. I was with Nicola Jarvis, my room-mate, and I said to her, 'If I make the duvet into a sail I'd probably go a lot quicker.'

So we both held on to our duvets, let them catch the wind and shot down the hill. It was such good fun that I went back to the top of the hill to do it again. Lloyd Upsdell had seen what I was doing and he came across.

'Can I have a go?'

'Okay.'

So Lloyd, who is about twelve stone, sat on my lap and held on to the top of the duvet. We tore down the hill. We were laughing as we rolled along, but we attracted some funny looks and the management weren't best pleased.

'You shouldn't be doing that,' said one official. 'It's against health and safety.'

'It was only a bit of fun,' I said.

'And how dare you lead this young boy astray?'

'He wanted to do it!' I said. The official wasn't having any of it, though, and Lloyd just stood there, killing himself laughing.

'Nothing to do with me,' he grinned.

Having fun with your team-mates and rivals like that is all part of being at a major games and although Birmingham wasn't a great event, the camaraderie between the athletes was brilliant. Staying with the amputee squad was good because everyone supported each other. The one thing we didn't have in Birmingham were national anthems at the medal ceremonies. It had been decided that they would take too long, but the Aussies decided to take things into their own hands. They got hold of a CD player and found a copy of 'Advance Australia Fair'. So whenever an Australian won a gold medal they would all pile over to the finishing line, stand up and sing the national anthem. They would refuse to move until they had finished singing. That started a trend and the guys in the amputee squad started doing it too. I won the 200 metres and waited for the medal presentation. Funnily enough, it was Dave Moorcroft, my boss, who presented me with it. Then Peter's guys all piped up and started singing the national anthem. The Aussies were up for anything so they joined in too and there was a French guy with a trumpet. He only knew a few notes but he did his best. We all stood singing 'God Save the Queen'. I don't usually sing during the medal ceremonies but I did on that occasion.

After that we joined in with the Aussies when they won a

medal. Most of us only knew the end bit to 'Advance Australia Fair' but we gave it a go and I remember humming along to 'La Marseillaise'. It made it so much more personal and, in a bizarre way, those karaoke anthems were the best part of the Games in Birmingham.

I don't usually get emotional in my own medal ceremonies but I do watching other people's. For instance, I cried when Steph Cooke won the gold medal in the modern pentathlon at the Sydney Olympics. I didn't know her at the time, but it was the way she won it, having to make up a 48 second deficit in the last event – the cross-country run – and the fact you had to scrape her off the ceiling afterwards. She was so busy running around seeing her friends and family that she didn't even have time for the BBC. I also got quite emotional watching the coxless fours win the rowing gold, but usually it's when my mates are involved that the tears come.

On the track, Birmingham was a bit mixed for me. I won the 200 metres, but came second to Leanne in the 400 and 800 metres. Almost as soon as I'd finished the 800, a guy from the team came up to me and said, 'Why did you choose those tactics?'

'Why do you think? Because I thought that was my best way of winning.'

It was just another example of how insensitive team officials can be after a race. I'd done a really fast first lap, then pulled out to let Leanne go through with the plan of kicking again. It was my only chance of winning gold because it was a very slow track. I couldn't go out slowly and hope to wind it up, but then you have someone saying, 'Why did you do that?'

The best thing you could say about Birmingham was it was not as bad as Atlanta. The Australians wouldn't stay in the accommodation and the crowd was made up of friends and family. If we held a games in this country now, I think we would get a lot more people attending on the back of Sydney, but crowds are a problem for athletics as a whole. Even mainstream events struggle to get people in unless they have someone like Marion Jones competing.

I went straight from Birmingham to the European Championships in Budapest where there was a women's 800 metres exhibition race. The four-star hotel we were staying in was a bit dilapidated but the people were lovely. I didn't get to see much of the city because I was only there for three days, but it was grey, depressing and very eastern bloc. I was just happy to be there because it had looked like I was going to miss my flight from Heathrow. Ric Cassell, the chairman of Wheelchair Racing, drove me down to the airport but we got stuck in horrendous traffic. We kept ringing to say we were going to be late and they asked us our details so they could have all the tags ready and waiting for us. Ric is a very calm bloke so when he started panicking I knew we were in trouble. We were meant to be parking in the long-term car park, but I told Ric to dump the car in short term. The people at the airport met us there and rushed us through. We got on with minutes to spare. After the stress of that journey and the exhaustion from competing at the Worlds, I just collapsed and went to sleep.

I'd calmed down a lot by the time the race came around. We spent a long time on the track beforehand and the rain was starting to dribble down. I went into the British tent with about half an hour to go before the race. Ric was there, talking to some of the British guys. I was really, really relaxed and put my head in my knees and fell asleep. Ric apparently came over to me at one point and then realised I was asleep.

'Is she coping all right?' an official asked.

'She's fine,' Ric said.

I was out for ten minutes but went on to win the race. That's happened to me a few times. I don't worry about not waking up in time for the race. It's like there's a built-in clock. It's a power nap really. I fell asleep in Sydney before my 200 metres final. I closed my eyes and switched my brain off. It only happens when I'm very relaxed and it's a good sign. If I'm asleep just before a race it means I'm going to do well. It's like a sixth sense. Sometimes you just absolutely know you are going to win. Unfortunately, that doesn't happen very often.

1998 was a good year for me both on and off the track. As well as winning the gold in Budapest, I also won the London Marathon and set a personal best of 1 hour 49.57 seconds for a marathon at Sempach. Having felt so down after Atlanta, I was back enjoying my athletics. It was also the year that Ian and I finally decided to get married. We'd been talking about it for ages but hadn't done anything about it. I didn't want a long engagement because I couldn't see the point and I didn't particularly like the idea of being Ian's fiancée. One day we were speaking on the phone and he said, 'Right, let's get engaged, get a ring and get married within a year.'

'Okay,' I said. 'You ring your mum and I'll ring mine.'

It may not have been the most romantic of proposals but my mum was very excited. My parents really like Ian so they were glad we were finally doing something about it.

'Have you got a ring?' Mum said.

'Not yet, no.'

Ian came down at the weekend and on the Saturday morning, he said, 'If you want a ring you've got to come now. We've got an hour.' Before we went out looking he asked me what sort of ring I wanted and jokingly announced that they were the only rings that I could look at otherwise I would take all day. Faith came with us to Birmingham's jewellery quarter and I remember passing one window full of rings that didn't match what I had said I wanted and Ian saying, 'You can't look in there.' We found a shop with some nice ones, but they were all three and five stones and I fancied four.

'Four's unlucky,' said the assistant.

'But the others don't look right,' I replied.

So we found another shop and got one with four stones. We thought we'd take our chances. Overall, including stopping to have an ice cream in the middle, we were out for about fifty minutes. Ian's very rational and couldn't see the point in traipsing around shops all day and then going back to the first one you'd been in, but I thought it was nice that we'd bought it together.

We decided to get married on 1 May 1999. We knew 2000 would be too busy with Sydney and we both felt it was the right time. The date was governed by our respective competition schedules and we settled on that one because it was two weeks after London and wouldn't disrupt the track season. Ian's main concern was the time of day we got married because he wanted to go training in the morning. Originally, there was going to be a track race on the day of the wedding and Ian reasoned that we could get them to put the races on in the morning, which would mean we could still make the wedding in the afternoon. I considered what he said and said to Mum, 'We could do it. Shower at the track, hairdresser's on the way home, make-up at home, stick my dress on, church.'

'You have got to be joking,' she said. Her face was a picture.

'I was,' I replied. 'Honest.'

The meeting was cancelled, which was probably just as well. If there had been a race on that day, Ian would definitely have entered. I recognise that might not be normal behaviour for most people, but it is for us. We think it's fine because our lives are centred on competing. I think we are lucky that we found each other because I don't imagine there are too many people who would feel the same way.

The time of the wedding was set for 2 p.m. at St John's Church in the centre of Cardiff. Ian stayed in a hotel the night before and went training on his own on the morning of the wedding. I went training too but had to go before 7 a.m. because I had to get ready. Mum was a bit exasperated with me, but she knew she wasn't going to change me. I've always gone training on Christmas Day, so she knows what I'm like. As I went out of the door, she said to me, 'Do not crash your chair, do not get a black eye and do not fall out. Understand? If you do I will never speak to you again.'

I was out for about thirty minutes and did five miles. Ian was intent on a full-blown training session, though, and spent ninety minutes flogging his guts out on the streets of Cardiff, just hours before he was due to get married. My main concern was his useless sense of direction. He didn't know that part of Cardiff very well and, being a typical bloke, would never stop to ask someone how to get back if he got lost. He'd prefer to find his own way using the sun or something equally daft.

'Take a map with you and take my phone,' I told him beforehand.

'I'll be fine, don't worry,' he said.

'If you get lost, ask someone,' I insisted.

'Yeah, right.'

'Promise.'

'Okay.'

I think he was quite conscious that it would annoy me intensely if he did something daft on that day and there wasn't a problem.

A sports photographer we know, Gray, had agreed to take our pictures and he got a few shots of me training when I looked like death warmed up. I'd organised a schedule for the day, which had prompted a lot of mickey-taking. Usually, I'm not the most organised of people, so the fact I had typed out a schedule and was trying to run the day with military precision surprised a lot of people. Sian, who is much more organised, thought it was hilarious and kept saying, 'I'm not doing that, it's not on the schedule.'

It was chaos in the house. A make-up artist friend from the BBC came to do my face and she also helped Sian and Nikki who were my bridesmaids. They had red dresses on and looked lovely. Mum had a big hat with feathers on it and Sian walked behind her flicking at them. 'Stop it! Stop it!' shouted Mum. I think she was more nervous than the rest of us. We were ready at 1.15 p.m. and Dad saw me in my wedding dress for the first time. 'You look nice,' he said, which was a lot for him because Dad doesn't usually say too much. We set off for the church and Dad forgot his hat. We didn't realise it until we saw our neighbours from across the road who were following us in their car, waving.

There was a slight problem in that the church bells had been sent away to Loughborough to be repaired. Somehow it didn't feel quite right to have a wedding without bells and I wondered whether we could do something with a CD. One of my friends from Loughborough, Joe Bidgood, had always been very musical and used to sort out the PA system for me when I did anything with the Rag committee at uni. So I rang Joe and he came down from his home in Aylesbury and said he thought he could stick a PA up in the bell tower and run a loop of wedding bells. 'We'll need to know the right cater, though, or it will sound stupid,' he said. So I ended up on the Internet, e-mailing *Ringing World* and asking what recording we needed. A few days before the wedding, Joe and his friend, Ben Andrews, went down to the church very early, wearing black boiler suits with identity badges and dark sunglasses, to put the PA in the belfry. They thought they were in a James Bond film or something. The vicar and bell captain humoured them, but they pulled it off. When we came around the corner to the church I rolled the window down because it was such a hot day and we could hear the bells. 'They sound nice,' I said and it took me a second to realise it was actually a recording. People kept asking us, 'How did you get the bells back?' And we had to say, 'We haven't.'

Walking down the aisle was quite emotional and when I got to the end, Ian turned and looked at me. 'You look beautiful,' he said. It's the most romantic thing he has ever said to me and he certainly hasn't said it since. I had told Gray that I absolutely didn't want to do any soft focus or kissy photographs. In fact, one of the best pictures we had was where Gray was trying to persuade us to do it and the look on my face says not a chance, while Ian is laughing.

The reception was in the Cardiff Bay Hotel. Mum had warned Dad not to make a long speech and not to say anything sickly or revolting. Then it was Ian's turn. He started off with a really bad joke. 'My speech has got to be like the bride's nightdress,' he said, 'long enough to cover everything but short enough to be interesting.' Everyone thought it was funny but I think most of them were drunk by then. Ian's best man was his brother, Stuart, and he gave a good speech with lots of amusing photos of Ian as a boy and plenty of embarrassing stories. We had a great party that night, but the next morning Ian and I were out training again.

We had dithered about whether we should go on honeymoon, but finally decided to go to Sempach in Switzerland, which we knew from competing in the marathon there. We were staying about ten metres off the course so that was great because it meant we knew exactly where to go training. We didn't have to waste time looking for new routes. Both of us took our laptop computers to do some work while we were there. That had caused a bit of mirth at the wedding. Ian's boss had said, 'You can't take your laptop on honeymoon. You need to learn how to relax.' But then his wife had butted in. 'That's rich considering you were in your room dialling into the office about half an hour ago!' Maybe we do have a problem with relaxing, but we thought it was great, sitting in an outdoor café, drinking coffee and eating cake as we both worked away on our laptops. It was the perfect honeymoon. And we only trained three hours a day so that was a bit wimpish really.

On the way home we had to make a detour to find Heinz Frei's house. Heinz had won the men's wheelchair race at the London Marathon that year but the glass trophy was so big that he hadn't been able to take it home. We decided to deliver it to him, so we set off for his village. It was not hard to find his street. Heinz is such a national hero in Switzerland that the street he lives on is named after him! His house was harder to find, but the local people had seen our racing chairs in the back of the car and realised we were looking for Heinz. They showed us the way. Unfortunately, there was nobody in so we went to the nearby hairdresser's to ask if anybody knew his whereabouts. Luckily, his wife was in there having her hair done so she came out and had a long chat with us. Not surprisingly, Heinz was out training, but we left the trophy and headed home. I dropped Ian at Hull so he could pick up his car and we set off in our separate directions. He went to Redcar and I went to Birmingham. It would be another eighteen months before we finally moved in together. That was hardly ideal but it wasn't planned and all good things come to those who wait!

Back in Birmingham I was growing frustrated with my job. British Athletics had been through financial ruin and my job had been pushed about all over the place. I had lots of different line managers with different aims and goals for me. That was frustrating and I felt as though I was being pulled in lots of different directions. Some regions were very successful in developing disability sport, but I got to the point where I didn't feel I was benefiting anybody. I was also doing a huge amount of travelling and decided I needed to leave if I wanted to get my head together for Sydney. So I went to see Dave Moorcroft and explained the situation. 'I'm sorry but I can't do this any more,' I said. As an ex-athlete, he understood. I felt that I had not achieved what I'd wanted to, but I knew I could not have done any more.

It is difficult to quantify achievement. Is it trying to develop the grass roots, as we had done in Birmingham, or is it performing at the élite end of the spectrum at Paralympics? Is it coaching kids or is it offering encouragement to people living with spina bifida like Harry's mum? You can't compare these things, but what is certain is that being in the public eye does put you in a privileged position. For example, I have been fortunate to be able to raise a lot of money for charity during my time as an athlete. I get numerous requests from charities asking if I will help them, and I pick those that I feel ethically comfortable with. I am not sure about some of the disability charities so I steer clear of those. I have to be happy with the way they raise money and how they use it.

I don't have a problem with *Children In Need*, even though it is very heart on the sleeve stuff, and I've done quite a few things for them. Raising money can be good fun. One year I had a lot of fun doing an Olympic Torch Fun Run at Cardiff Athletics Stadium with Steve Cram and a bunch of kids. I remember sitting in my chair and my shoelace was undone. Steve quipped, 'Hey, Tanni, you'd better do that up or you'll trip up in a minute.' Of course, I couldn't very well trip up, so I jokingly told him, 'Get lost.' Then a few seconds later the lace got caught in my wheel and I did go flying out of my chair!

One charity I feel very attached to is the RNLI. My Uncle Ivor worked in the shipping business and was heavily into protecting people on boats. Dad got involved through him and then I started raising money for them. I've done the London Marathon for them twice and they have thanked me by naming one of their boats after me. I went down to name the boat the *Tanni Grey* and bashed a bottle of champagne on the side. I think Mum thought I was having an ocean-going liner named in my honour, but it was only a dinghy. I got to drive it and one of the guys in the crew asked if I liked the water. 'I can't stand it,' I replied. I can swim okay, but there's something about the sea. It's such a long way down.

I have also supported the People's Dispensary for Sick Animals (PDSA). I love animals so am very happy to help the PDSA in any way I can. One of my regrets about being an athlete is that all the travelling means I can't have a dog. My parents have always had dogs and they used to be protective of me when I was growing up. It was as if they sensed there was something different about me. We had a mother and daughter called Du and Pip when we were little. Du was completely docile. Sian once crawled across the carpet and stuck both her fingers up her nose but Du didn't flinch. She would often lay on the tiles in the lounge because they caught the sun in the summer, and I'd sometimes lie down next to her and go to sleep. Pip was more aggressive. When I was still walking, I was struggling to get to the end of the drive one day when some kids from across the road started throwing snowballs. Pip got very angry about that and chased after them.

Not long after Barcelona I found myself at London Zoo. They had decided to name a newly born giraffe after me. That was really sweet and I went along to meet my namesake. Sian said it should have been a monkey rather than a giraffe, but I had a good day as I met Tanni and her brother, Graham Gooch, and sister, Sally Gunnell!

When I have retired and I look back at my career, perhaps then I'll be able to say what my greatest achievement has been. But I don't think in those terms. I hope that maybe I've helped change the way athletes are treated and I think having a high profile helps in that respect. Some people on the team say to me, 'Why do you get asked to do so much?' and I'm sure others think, oh, God, it's her again. But I have worked hard for it; nothing is handed to you on a plate. I do think disabled athletes are getting more recognition now, but they have to work hard because very few athletes make much money.

What have I achieved? It's a difficult question. I've never let my disability get in the way because there is nothing I can do about it, but I don't consider that an achievement. What I do believe is that if you have the will, the luck, the time and the energy, you can achieve everything. Whether you can walk or not does not come into it.

Chapter Ten

The Return of the
Golden Girl

W HEN the sun finally set on the year 2000 my life had changed forever. It was a momentous year, but it was one of mixed emotions – highs and lows, fears and dreams, pain and pleasure. My reputation was at an all-time high, but the previous twelve months had been some of the hardest I had known.

Everything seemed to be moving along smoothly at the start of the year. I was building up for the Sydney Paralympics in the autumn and looking forward to Sian's wedding to James in February. I like having James around because it means Sian orders his life instead of mine. My sister is the most organised person you could imagine and will buy someone's birthday present six months in advance, whereas I'll go out and get something the day before. That New Year's Eve there was something wrong with the mashed potato she was making for dinner, so James and I both made suggestions. Sian half-jokingly told James off and I started laughing. 'Don't you start either,' she snapped at me. James and I share that common bond – Sian never stops nagging either of us! She met him when she was working as a nurse and James was training to be a surgeon. I think that's why he's got a good sense of humour – you have to in that line of work just to survive. He has been good for Sian because she is much more relaxed now.

We were all excited about the wedding, which was going to be in the same church where Ian and I had got married, but a week beforehand Mum was rushed into hospital. She has a problem with her blood. That Christmas she had a cold and was warned not to come into contact with any people who had chicken pox, shingles or a cold. Unfortunately, when we went home for the holidays, Sian had chicken pox, James had shingles and I had a bad cold! That didn't help her condition and she grew progressively worse.

On the night she was admitted to hospital as an emergency, I'd been out doing an interview for BBC Radio Wales and had decided to go for a curry with some of the production guys I knew. I rang home at around 9 p.m. and was surprised to hear Sian answer the phone. I knew straightaway that something was wrong – it was the tone of Sian's voice.

'What are you doing there?' I asked.

'It's Mum,' Sian said. 'She's not very well and we're taking her into hospital.'

'What's wrong?' I could feel the panic mounting as I spoke.

'Meet us at casualty.'

I got in the car and drove home like a complete nutcase. I got there just in time to see Mum being put in the back of an ambulance. We followed her in my car. Mum didn't realise what was going on because she was so ill. She was struggling to breathe because her lungs were full of a gloopy substance and that had affected her blood and made it more imbalanced. The doctors put her on really strong antibiotics and started giving her lots of blood as soon as they could.

Sian and I sat in the family room with my Dad. That's the room where they take the relatives to keep them away from the ward while they give them the good or the bad news. It was very depressing and frightening. There were lots of happy posters on the wall in a vain attempt to make you feel better, and on the table in front of us was a massive box of Quality Street. I was absolutely famished because I hadn't eaten anything so I started having a few.

'You can't eat all the sweets,' said Sian.

'Yes, I can,' I replied. 'That's what they're here for.'

A nurse Sian knew popped her head around the door at that point. 'Do you want a cup of tea?' she asked.

'Yes, please,' I replied.

Sian told me I shouldn't have had a cup of tea but if it was a trying time for Dad and me, it must have been horrific for her. She was due to get married in a few days and Mum was seriously ill in hospital. Dad was upset, but kept a calm exterior and we all started arguing about little things that weren't important because, deep down, we were scared.

'I'm going to cancel the wedding,' said Sian.

'You can't do that,' I told her. 'Mum will be all right. You'll see. She'll come out for the service and it will all be okay.'

The human mind works in strange ways and we were so stressed that we started laughing about stupid things.

'Mum hasn't finished decorating the cake,' lamented Sian. 'What are we going to do?'

'I'm sure there is someone else in Cardiff who can ice a wedding cake,' I said, putting another toffee in my mouth. Then I looked up. I couldn't believe my eyes. There, on the wall, was a poster advertising someone who did cake decorations. 'See!' I said. 'I told you.' We both started laughing out loud. Somehow that poster helped us to stop panicking.

Mum ended up having to have her spleen out. It's meant to weigh seven ounces but hers was eight-and-a-half pounds which shows how bad it was. When I was growing up, she always told me to ask doctors questions but when it came to herself, she didn't want to know. She could have saved herself a lot of worry if she had asked the doctors more questions earlier on. To everyone's relief, she did come out for the wedding, but she was doped up on all sorts of drugs and struggling a bit. One of the guests at the wedding, who didn't know what had happened, came up to her and said, 'You look terrible.' I managed not to say anything but what I really thought was shut up! It was a hard day for Mum. Sian looked beautiful and I think that, apart from all the panic leading up to it, they had a great day.

Mum slowly got better, life returned to normal, and I settled back in to training. I had a bad London Marathon because of a puncture and came second, but then set a personal best in the Lake Sempach Marathon when I came sixth in a time of 1 hour 48.5 minutes. Ian knew early that year that he was not going to make it to Sydney. His chance had gone at Atlanta when he might have done so much better but for all the extra problems surrounding us at that time. But if he was disappointed about Sydney it didn't stop him from helping me. I remember sitting down one night with him and Martin and talking about what I could do at the Paralympics.

'I reckon I could do two golds and two silvers if everything goes well,' I said. After Atlanta I wanted to go to the Games thinking of every different scenario.

'Don't be daft,' said Ian.

'What?'

'You can do four golds.'

'No, I can't.'

'Yes, you can.'

We proceeded to have an argument about what I could hope for, while Martin sat there with a wry smile on his face.

Not long before I was due to go to Sydney for the Olympics, I began to get worried about my own health. I had started to feel very tired and was sleeping for twelve hours a day. I knew something was wrong and, because of Mum's problems, I started to get a bit paranoid. I'd read up on her illness and knew that excessive tiredness was one of the symptoms and that people in their early thirties were particularly prone to getting it. I began imagining all sorts of scenarios and so I went to the doctor to have some blood tests.

It was also around that time that I started keeping a diary. I had kept one in an ad hoc manner leading up to major games. So much can happen that it is easy to forget some things and I wanted to be able to look back on Sydney in future years and remember. At the time I didn't imagine that there would be so much to write about, both good and bad, but it became part of my daily routine. This is how I saw the few months beforehand and the Sydney Paralympics.

Friday, 11 August

I travelled out to the Swedish Elite Games on my own. I need to get some fast times on the track and also prepare for the Olympic trials. Nobody else from the team wanted to come out with me, which is a shame because the track is so fast. I'm staying in a tiny room at the Spar Hotel. When I got here, I met up with the Irish girls, Patrice Dockery, Colette O'Reilly and Mairead Farquarson. Tried to call Ian a few times but he was permanently engaged. The journey seemed to take forever and I'm so tired, but I don't get the results of my blood tests until I get home.

Monday, 14 August

My races over the weekend were a bit up and down. On the Saturday the weather was quite chilly and there was a lot of swirling wind in the stadium. In the 1500 metres, I led out for the sprint, but didn't pick up too well in the finishing straight. Lou Sauvage and Patrice Dockery came past and beat me. In the 100 metres my first five pushes were poor and the time was not great. That was annoying because ever since January I've been working hard on my starts. I don't think I'll be able to rely on my top speed to win the 100 metres in Sydney – I need a really good start too. Tried to think of lots of reasons why I have spent so much time working on my starts and they are still not quite there. The trouble is my arms are too long! When you push you are holding the rim of the wheel for a short space of time so by the time I have got my arms down, round and back up again, some of the other girls are on their second push. I need to improve and have spent months and months working at it. I hate that sort of training so I've been doing a bit of start work in every single session. It doesn't seem to have made much difference. The track in Gothenburg is the same sort that we will be racing on in Sydney and I'd been hoping for a quick time.

The 200 metres was into a head wind and you just couldn't tell which way it was going to blow. But just before the 400 the wind dropped and the flags were barely moving. As I was warming up I figured that if I was going to push a good time anywhere then it would be here. There was a random draw on the lanes for the final and I drew the outside lane, which I wasn't happy about. Usually I like to use the others in the race to 'pick off' but at least it meant I couldn't do anything apart from race – if I can't see the others I can't worry about them. The four stages of the race all went well. It was a maximum sprint for the first 100 metres. Then I tried to relax and pick up my elbows, and almost slow my pushing down for the second 100 while maintaining my speed, followed by kicks at 200 and 300 metres. It's the same technique I use for any 400 metre race. I split it into four sections and focus on each one individually. In the 400 metres the idea is not to tie up in the last 100 like runners often do. I crossed the line first and looked up at the time: 57.00! It was a new world record. It was almost like the race had been run in slow motion. I'd looked at my clock and knew from my splits that it was going to be close to 57 seconds. Two years ago I never thought I'd get the 400 metre world record back from Leanne Shannon. That began to change through the season when I started clocking fast times but you can never tell what will happen in a race like that. I had come close several times and I thought that was all I was going to do.

The BBC called me while I was at the hotel. One of the girls I used to work with at the Disability Programmes Unit has suggested that they may want me to do a Paralympic diary for them. I need to think about this one. It could be a good idea, but I am not sure that I am ready for everyone to see the day to day ups and downs and how I deal with them. I don't know whether I want to inflict myself on the public in that way.

Had a couple of extra days in Gothenburg. It was a struggle to get around because there were so many cobbles everywhere and I nearly fell out of my chair a few times. There's lots in the paper about the Irish peace agreement. The Australians and the Canadians are talking about setting up an International Racing Association. They don't understand why we can't call it the IRA!

Can't stop thinking about the 800 metres demo race at the Olympics. I know it's going to be a very tough one.

Training at the Ullevi Stadium is good – Mondo surface so all the times are going well. The Russians have been here too and were doing relay training for three hours *non-stop*. It is such a different world for these guys.

Thursday, 17 August

Travelled to Switzerland for the Swiss Nationals and the Olympic trials and seem to be staying in a Catholic respite home for disabled people. The nuns are very sweet but it's a little strange being woken at 6 a.m. by bells calling us to worship. A lot of them seem quite intrigued by what we do because many of the people they look after are the long-term sick or severely impaired. I think we are something of a novelty for them. I have tried practising my French on them. I have started taking lessons because I think it might come in useful for a future career and for travelling, so it is nice to try it out on people who can speak it properly. They seem to be able to understand me, just about, so that's good.

Friday, 18 August

The first round of the Olympic trials ended up with some seriously tactical racing. Cheri Becerra (USA) went off really fast and I tried to chase her, while Madeline Nordlund (SWE) sat with Edith Hunkeler (SUI), and then tried to sprint. Ariadne

Hernandez (MEX) and Lily Angrenny (GER) were about six metres behind, but Lily was working hard to get closer. I think Cheri is trying to see what she can do on her own because she wants to push quicker than Lou, and I think she and Chantal are going to try to run a world record sometime soon. Lou didn't have to race in the trials at all because, as the host nation, the Aussies get a free place and they gave it to her. I thought that was really ethical. Lou has won every demo race since 1992, so the Aussies could have given the free place in the final to one of their young girls and made Lou qualify. They didn't do that because they decided any Aussie who makes it to the final should make it on merit. Not many other countries would do that.

Saturday, 19 August

I had to get up very early to organise transport for the other British athletes, even though I wasn't competing until late morning. The coach that UK Athletics sent speaks no French and he doesn't know who to speak to in order to get things done. Nicola (Jarvis) has got early heats which is so tough – they arrived late last night. So I ended up having to fix transport or she wouldn't have got to the track in time.

I was very, very ill before my race. I must have thrown up ten times. It's the worst I've ever been. Usually it's just once and that's it. This time I couldn't leave the toilet. I was in there for an hour solid. Every time I came out, I felt it coming again and ended up rushing back in! I have thought about every eventuality but making it through matters so much.

For the second round I had to wear Nicola's racing suit. After the first round there were all sorts of complications because one of the American guys evoked a rule that is hardly ever used about wearing national kit. It actually states in the rules that you have to wear official national kit to compete in the trials, but the trouble is we don't have official British kit unless we are at the Paralympics or World Championships. I had been racing in my own kit, and planned to wear my blue Nike suit. I don't carry any other stuff with me as it goes against my sponsorship agreement. As I was the only British athlete in that race, I figured that would be okay. But then I checked the rules and, although they were ambiguous, realised that if I was to abide by the letter of the law, I needed something with GB on it. The only thing I could do was borrow Nicola's kit. She'd done the 100 metres that morning, wearing her Atlanta kit. We spent a long time discussing what I should do and she said, 'There's no point you getting disqualified on a technicality.' She was right. That would have been horrific. So I raced in her Lycra. I guess it shows how well we get on that I would race in it, and she would let me! It wasn't too bad and could definitely have been worse. Better to share a top with Nicola than Chris Hallam! It all helped me take my mind off the race, so that was one positive aspect of it all. It was good of Nicola to help me out and it caused quite a laugh.

The draw for the semi-final was pinned on the results board when I arrived at the track and again I got a really good deal. I was in the first semi, but a lot of the sprinters had been drawn in the second race. I had a talk with Cheri beforehand and discussed the possibilities of how it would work for us both to get through. Cheri went off fast, just as she had done in the first round, and I went with her. She pulled *me* along and I watched everyone else to make sure I knew where the attacks might come from. It worked. We both made it.

The other semi was tough with Jean Driscoll, Chantal Peticlerc,

Waikako Tscheido, Jessica Galli, Madeline Nordlund, Edith Hunkeler, Patrice Dockery and Kristie Skelton. Patrice didn't make it through – she was devastated. She has improved so much this season which has been fantastic, but it was such a tough draw.

S4C came over to Switzerland to interview me. I was a little stressed beforehand – something to do with the race I think, but I was fine afterwards.

Sunday, 20 August

The weather was hot for the rest of the weekend, so much so that my tyres would barely stick because the glue had melted. I also got pulled in for a doping test at the end of the 400 metres. We didn't have a female official with us so Nicola came with me. The doping room was inaccessible so I had to be carried up the steps.

Spoke to the estate agent's on the phone. We're trying to sell Ian's house in Redcar and get a bigger place, but it seems to be pure hassle. The story changes all the time and now they want us to move quickly. In retrospect, I don't think this is the best time in the world to have decided to move house!

I'd agreed to give Nicola a lift home from the airport in Newcastle as my flight was due in just before hers. Unfortunately, hers was delayed which meant wandering around Newcastle Airport for two hours with nothing to do.

Tuesday, 22 August

Got results of my blood tests back. They can't find anything. It feels good to know for sure that everything is OK.

I was listening to Sue Cook on the radio and the guy who has designed the walking-out kit was on. He mentioned that he was doing the kit for both the Olympics and Paralympics. It was the first time I'd heard the Olympics and Paralympics linked together like that. The Paralympians are always keen to use the Olympic link, but it is not often reciprocated. Went to Leeds to get fitted for our Paralympic kit. The changing rooms were all full, so I just got undressed in the middle of the warehouse. That was probably a shock to some of the people there but when you race, you get used to changing in the back of cars and in the middle of fields. My trousers didn't fit. I had to have a size 14 jacket because my shoulders are so wide, but I needed size 10 trousers. They'd given me 14. They'd run out of women's kit by that time, so I ended up with a pair of bloke's trousers. We were given loads of stuff – a stack of T-shirts, walking-out suits, tracksuits, socks. We even had black M&S knickers, although they gave me size 16, so I gave them away. The suits are really nice – navy with a blue stripe. They might be a bit formal for the opening ceremony but it's great to have trousers – being in a wheelchair and wearing skirts does not work. The Aussies are having really jazzy khaki jeans and turquoise and orange sweatshirts. It's amazing what our Olympic team get given. They won't need to take anything with them to the Games. They even get their shower gel and toothbrush provided!

Wednesday, 23 August

Needed to get away so have come to France with Ian for a few days. I also want to spend some time with him before I go away to Australia. We went through the Channel Tunnel, which was very quick, and then I drove in France. We went down to Bethune for a few days. Ian has to do some work and then we can rest and train.

Thursday, 24 August

I got a call from Mervyn who is one of the track officials. He wants me to have some of his collection of memorabilia. Last year I was racing at the Nationals at Stoke Mandeville when there was an announcement over the Tannoy saying, 'Can Tanni Grey please come to the officials area?' I thought, what have I done now? You only get pulled in when you've done something wrong. I thought John Tanner, one of the technical officials, would be waiting for me. John's a brilliant guy but very strict. He tells you off in a calm and dignified way that makes you feel about two inches tall and makes you realise that you should know better. But it was Mervyn who wanted to see me, not John. Mervyn had got a spare set of gold, silver and bronze medals from the Paralympics when they were held at Stoke Mandeville. He gave them to me which was really nice of him. It means I actually have one more gold than people think!

Now Mervyn says there are some other things that he wants me to have. One of the things is a book from when Sir Ludwig Guttmann was setting up the original spinal injury games. There are lots of documents, too. 'They'll mean more to you than they will to my family,' he said. 'I know you'll look after them.' He is so sweet. He was at some of the very first Games that I competed in and is still there as a volunteer. I must get in touch when I am back.

Tuesday, 29 August

When Ian is in France he often stays at a chateau on the outskirts of Bethune. There is a Commonwealth war graveyard next to it. Stacks of British soldiers are buried there. Before we went, I'd been listening to a programme on First World War diaries on Radio Four and they were talking about a specific regiment who had been based in the area, many of whom were buried in Bethune. So while Ian was working, I went to have a look at the graveyard. Then we decided to go to Ypres. I've always wanted to go to the war memorial there and so we went last night. Unfortunately, we had a row on the way because I nearly got us killed. I was in the wrong lane, didn't have the right of way, and tried to turn left. A bus almost hit us. It was a very close shave. The bus driver was very angry, but Ian was laughing and saying, 'Tourist, tourist!' as he pointed at me. We'd been driving around Ypres for over an hour at that point. We thought there would be a sign saying 'War Memorial', but I didn't realise there'd be signs for different memorials every couple of kilometres. I was shocked at just how many cemeteries there were. We stopped at one and there were 15,000 names on it and that wasn't even the main one. As fate would have it, the road we swerved down to avoid the bus was actually the one we were looking for. I'd seen the cemetery on television, but it was a humbling experience to stand there. Thousands of names were engraved into the bridge that straddled the road. Most of them were privates and lower ranking soldiers. I read the memorial book and that was quite an emotional experience. There were messages in it from everyone from seven-year-olds through to veterans who had fought there and returned to pay their respects.

There were two guys from the local fire service waiting by the entrance. They were chatting away and one of them was having a smoke. Then they looked at their watches and realised it was nearly 6 p.m. They suddenly sparked into very formal action and played 'The Last Post'. I bawled my eyes out. Afterwards, I ended up speaking to a guy who ran a memorial fund there and he told me that there were people who lived nearby who go and stand there every night to listen to that poignant call. It was eerie.

I have always liked history but the fact that Mum's dad, Dubby Jones, fought in the First World War makes it mean a bit more. My grandfather was sent home from battle because he was injured and I still treasure the whistle he gave me from the war with 1913 engraved on it. Remembrance Day was always a big occasion in our house but whenever Mum asked Dubby Jones about the war, he would always change the subject.

Thursday, 31 August

Interviewed for something called the People's Award. It's for contribution to sport rather than sporting achievement. I'm not sure how I feel about that. I unpacked all my kit and found that I don't have a GB top. I rang the BPA to let them know and they are sorting one out for me and will make sure that I have one.

Thursday, 7 September

Home in Redcar and just relaxing before I go off to the Olympics. There is so much to organise. I've got a huge list of everything I need to take and am slowly working my way through it.

Tuesday, 19 September

Got into Sydney this morning and am staying at the Regent Hotel. It is very nice, but it is hard to get to the village from here. Most of the other Paralympic athletes are staying with their Olympic teams, apart from us and the Americans. I get the impression that someone is worried that if I do well in the Olympics demo race, I am not going to stay around for the Paralympics. I can see why it causes problems. The Paralympics are trying hard to create their own identity and then there is a group of us who have the opportunity to compete at both. A couple of years ago one of the team administrators told me they thought I shouldn't try for both. But I said to someone from the BPA, 'Anybody would want to race at the Olympics if they had the chance.'

'I wouldn't,' he said.

'Yeah, right.'

On the way through Heathrow, Ian and I got upgraded by an airline official. Very nice. Met at the airport by Jim and Ian, two volunteers who are a bit like an old married couple. They jokingly bicker all the time but are absolutely fantastic. The first thing Jim said as we came through was that Jason Queally had won the first medal for Britain at the Olympics. We also found that Louise Ramsey from the BOA had made sure we were on the system for accreditation to make our processing easier.

Thursday, 21 September

Took the bus and the train to the village today. I also had to find some glue – one of the discs on my wheels is starting to pull apart and I don't want to race on my tri-spokes. I have pushed really well on the discs all year and don't want to change now. With tri-spokes there are gaps between each of the spokes and you can put your hand through there by mistake. I've done that a few times when I've been going fast and have badly damaged my hands. It's not worth it. After years of not being superstitious, I don't want to race on tri-spokes now. Max Jones, the team Performance Director, invited me to the team meeting tonight which was nice of him. Lorna Boothe, one of the officials from the Olympic team, is trying to sort out lots of stuff for me. She is very helpful and supportive. She 'walked me through' in Athens at the Worlds in 1997 and, having been an athlete, she knows what it is like. Her sister is a wheelchair-user too, so she is more understanding than most.

I went to the team doctor because I needed to get a needle. All needles have to be signed out.

'Is it for insulin?' he asked.

'No, it's for glue,' I said. He looked slightly bemused. I think he thought I was mad. 'I need to inject it into my wheel where the rim's cracked,' I explained.

Friday, 22 September

I sat in the sun in the village, having a coffee with Ian and fixing my wheel with the needle and glue. Very civilised. Steve Redgrave was there with his wife. 'How come you've got to fix your wheel?' Steve asked.

'There are only so many sets of wheels I can bring with me and these are the ones I like best,' I told him. 'I have to race on these.'

I don't know whether he was aware of it, but lots of athletes were walking past, casting sly looks at him and then chatting to each other. One young swimmer came up to him.

'I just want to tell you we're all going to be there, supporting you tomorrow,' he said. 'Good luck.'

'Thanks very much,' Steve said.

I don't believe in luck. There's no such thing. It is either going to happen for him or it isn't. So I didn't say anything to him apart from, 'Have a good one.'

Saturday, 23 September

Ian woke me early so that we could watch the rowing on the television. I felt incredibly tired and struggled to get up. It was a great race and Steve Redgrave winning a fifth successive gold medal was superb for team morale. Ian kept telling me not to shout at the television. 'That's not going to help him,' he said.

Monday, 25 September

Stayed in the hotel today while Ian went to meet someone from ICI. I tried to find somewhere to send e-mails. I complain when I bring my computer with me because I have to lump it around and then I complain when I don't. I went swimming in the open-air pool at the hotel. Everyone thought I was mad because it was only 12 degrees. Mad dogs and Englishmen – or Welsh women.

Tuesday, 26 September

Two days until the Olympic final. The tension is beginning to mount. The weather was bad today but I don't want to know what it's going to be like for the race. You can't change the weather so why worry.

Wednesday, 27 September

There was a meeting in the village tonight. We thought that it was going to be a technical meeting, but it turned into an athletes versus International Paralympic Committee debate. There are a lot of rumours flying around that wheelchair racing will not be included at the Athens Olympics in 2004. Lots of other disability categories look at us and understandably get a bit moany because we always have demo status. So far disability sport is allowed one event at the Olympics and there are other sports pushing hard to get the place for Athens. Visually impaired running, swimming, tennis and basketball are all keen. The advantage we have over sports such as basketball is that we take up a few minutes of the schedule.

I also think the fact that we are different but don't look 'too disabled' makes people comfortable. People want to know that there is a disability but they don't want to know what it is. That is why lots of people aren't comfortable with other categories because the athletes look different. Maybe that's not aesthetically pleasing to some people.

Thursday, 28 September

Race day. I stayed in bed until 9.30 a.m. and managed to eat
some breakfast, which was good! The waitress gave me some
bread wrapped in a napkin to take with me to the race. I managed
to eat a little more at 2 p.m. and then had some coffee.

Went by bus and train to the village and made sure that I was
there very early. Went to the store room where we are keeping
our chairs and waited there. I just need to be close to the stadium.
Charlie, who looks after all the kit, had given us the combination
to the padlock so we could get in and out when we wanted. It's
also the place where they keep the unused mattresses. I was
feeling very lethargic in the early afternoon and they looked very
comfortable so I said to Ian, 'I think I'll have a lie down on
there.' He gave me a leg up and I pulled a blanket over my head
and went to sleep. Charlie came in at one point, looking for
some boxes.

'Shhh,' said Ian. 'Tanni's asleep.'

'Where?' said Charlie.

'Up there.' Ian pointed and Charlie saw a bundle of rags.

'Tch,' Charlie sighed. 'The life of a world-class athlete.'

I was sick at about 5 p.m. Lorna is ill so she can't walk me
through from the village to the track. That's a shame. Ian has
decided not to warm up with me. He didn't think it was fair
because none of the other girls had wheelchair athletes to warm
up with. He was fantastic and sorted out a lot of things for me
before the race.

The Aussies are really strict about branding on chairs. Every
sticker has to be scratched off or covered up. It's a pain in the
neck. Even my gloves had to be taped up. One guy took a Stanley
knife to Lou's chair to remove a sticker that was all of half a

centimetre wide. Lou is usually fairly stroppy but she just sat there and took it. I thought it was wrong. 'Can you stop doing that?' I said to the guy. 'I don't think anyone's going to see that one, are they?' The last thing you need before an Olympic final is someone taking a knife to your chair.

The race itself was a strange one. Cheri Becerra and Chantal Peticlerc went off fast but they seemed to bottle it 100 metres in. If they'd kept going I think one of them would have won, but they dropped back into the pack and came nowhere. Lou won again. I was fourth. Did a post-race interview for the BBC with Chris Boxer. They showed the race live and did re-runs. If this is anything to go by, the Paralympics are going to be really good.

Friday, 29 September

Left Sydney for the Gold Coast in Queensland where the holding camp for the Paralympics is based. Ian has gone home. I feel sad and I know I am going to miss him. A lot of people are surprised that he's not going to be at the Paralympics, but we decided it would be daft for him to use up all his holiday from work when it is all going to be on television. I wouldn't be able to see him that much and I can speak to him on the phone, so it will be fine.

Saturday, 30 September

I slept well last night, the best since I've been here. I relaxed a bit and watched Chris Boardman do his time trial on the TV. We have a live BBC feed in the hotel, which is great. Watching Chris reminded me of the time when we were in Monte Carlo for the Manchester Olympic bid in 1993. He'd just signed for the GAN team and went out riding every day in his new team kit. One day a British supporter came rushing into the hotel. 'Boardman's been knocked off his bike by a car,' he yelled. Cue pandemonium. About seventy Brits who were there supporting the bid tore out of this posh hotel. I stayed because there was nothing I could do to help. These people were literally fighting each other to treat Chris. Then, after a while, they began trudging back in.

'Is everything all right?' I asked. 'How's Chris?'

'Oh, it wasn't him after all,' said one. 'Just some other guy in a GAN shirt.'

'What happened?'

'I don't know,' he said. 'We all just left him.' They had, too. Once they knew it wasn't Chris, they turned around and left this poor guy lying in a heap!

Sunday, 1 October

The last day of the Olympic Games. Audley Harrison got gold in the boxing. A good way to round off a great Olympics.

Monday, 2 October

I can't believe the television over here or, probably, how sad I am. I've been watching episodes of *Sons and Daughters* and *The Sullivans* that I saw twenty years ago at home! Bizarrely, the guy who plays Phillip in *Neighbours* and is married to Julie is also in *Sons and Daughters* where he has a wife called Julie. Oh, dear! I think I watch too much TV. At least there is the destruction of Summer Bay in *Home and Away* to look forward to. Apparently, they are going to blow it up.

Spent the rest of the day unpacking and doing my French. I tried not to take over too much room for when Nicola arrives. The weather is great for training.

Wednesday, 4 October

The rest of the team arrived today and I feel much happier. I've been really looking forward to it. Went out training with Dan Saddler, which was fantastic. Dan tailors his training to suit mine. I wanted to do some fast sessions, so he towed me round. Nicola was impressed with the space I'd left in the room. Usually the first thing we do is decide which bits of furniture we don't need and chuck them out. This had all been done before we moved in – the hotel had planned things really well.

Thursday, 5 October

Went to the track and did an interview with *The Australian*, the national newspaper. On the way back we saw an accident involving a taxi that was driving one of the quadriplegic rugby players around. We were on a bus and saw this taxi tipped over on its side with smoke coming out of it. One coach said, 'Don't worry, it's not one of ours.'

'Yes, it is,' I said.

'No,' he insisted. 'It's not an athlete so we shouldn't get involved.'

I couldn't believe him. Neither could Danny. He rushed out of the bus and sprinted over to help. I thought that was amazing. Danny lost his arm in a car crash and yet the first thing he did was tear over to help. The guy was lucky. There was a bit of blood around, but he escaped with just cuts and bruises.

Went out in the afternoon with Nicola, Dan, Danny Crates and Lloyd Upsdell, just to get away from it all for a couple of hours.

Saturday, 7 October

Day off from training. Had a massage and then went to a wildlife park in the afternoon for about two hours.

Sunday, 8 October

During training I felt a pain down my left side. It was a bit sore getting into my chair. Two months ago I'd had some pain but put it down to the fact I'd been doing a lot of driving. I thought it was where the seat belt was cutting into me. In Sydney I've been doing a lot of speed work and I thought that might be the cause. At the training track, I went into one of the tents to get out of the sun and check my side. That was when I felt the lump in my left breast. My heart raced and I took a few deep breaths. Nicola and Karen Lewis were both there. I felt terrible.

'I think I've found a lump,' I said to Nicola.

'What do you mean?'

'Well, I'm not sure.'

Nicola came closer to me and I asked her to check as well.

'Go and see the doctor right now,' said Karen.

'No, I'll be all right,' I said. I tried to laugh it off but I felt physically sick. I didn't know it at the time, but Karen has had personal experience of cancer in her family and she was adamant that I go and see the doctor. She was literally shouting at me to get it checked out.

'I'm going to go training first,' I said. 'There's nothing I can do about it at the moment.' The team doctor, Mark Brooke, was at the training session so I found him and said, 'I need to come and see you later. I think I've found something.'

He was very calm. 'Come and see me as soon as you get back from training,' he said softly.

I tried to do some 150 metres and some pick-ups, which are acceleration drills, but none of it was very good. My mind was a whirlwind. I wanted to go. Nicola and Karen came back with me on the bus. The training track is about twenty minutes away from where we are staying but the journey felt like it was one of the longest I have been on. I went over it again and again in my mind. Part of me wanted to know what was wrong and part of me didn't, for fear of what it might be. It was with a lot of trepidation that I arrived at the doctor's clinic. I had mentally geared myself up to accepting that I had a lump. Don't worry, I told myself without much success. If there is a problem, I'll get it sorted. That's all there is to it. Mark was really nice to me. There is a great relationship between the team and the doctors in Sydney.

'Would you prefer a female medic to examine you?' Mark said.

'No, it's okay,' I said. 'I'm happy for you to do it.'

He put some screens around us. The room doubles as the physio's room and there were some people in there getting their massages. Mark sat down beside me and felt around. Then he looked at me. That moment seemed to last forever. 'You're right,' he said. 'There are two lumps there.' I instantly burst into tears. I had expected him to say one, but to hear two blew my mind. I'd wanted him to say, 'You're completely imagining it,' even though I knew I wasn't. I'd somehow prepared myself for him saying there was a lump, but when he said there were two the emotion just came pouring out. 'It will be okay, Tanni,' he said.

I could have agreed to take some antibiotics for the pain and waited until I get home to be diagnosed properly, but I want it doing now. I want to get checked out because, if there is something wrong, I wanted to be in a position to do something about it. You hear all these horror stories about people who ignore things and then find it's too late when they go to the doctor six weeks later. If there is anything that needs doing, I want it doing as soon as possible.

Nicola was waiting for me outside the room.

'What did he say?' she asked.

I was in a daze. 'I can't remember,' I said. Panic or what. One of the PR girls spoke to me at that point. She was telling me about the great pre-Games coverage that the team was already getting. She didn't know there was anything wrong and was trying to sort out the arrangements for some interviews. Nicola made me go back and see Mark.

'I'm terribly sorry,' I said. 'I've forgotten what you actually told me.'

'That's perfectly understandable,' he replied. And so he went through it all again. He was very patient. I went back and told Nicola, to make sure that I got it right. I also spoke to Vicky Tolfrey, one of the basketball staff. I had worked with her over a number of years on sports science testing and knew that I could talk to her. She reminded me that her mum worked with breast cancer and gave me her number. 'Ring her,' she said, 'if there is anything you need to know.' I didn't, but it was nice to know I could.

Nicola offered to come with me to the hospital but I decided that it would be better for us both if she stayed at the complex. Mark drove me to a private hospital. That's one of the benefits we have. Everyone on the team has private health insurance while we are away. I had to have an ultrasound which was very tickly and a bit painful. The girl there told me they would only do a mammogram if they thought it was serious. Then, after seeing the results, she proceeded to tell me she thought I'd need one! Another doctor did a breast examination and I had to wait for the results. I was glad Mark was there. We ended up having tea and biscuits and joking about things that weren't funny at all. The fact is I was in hospital and very scared. Finally the doctor came out. 'I think you have got cysts,' he said. The relief was huge, but his diagnosis isn't definite. I still need it checked out. The hospital gave me some medicine. I have to break up the tablets because I can't swallow them without bringing them back up. They taste awful.

For some reason I thought it was important for Ian Campbell, (we always call him Doc Campbell) our racing co-ordinator to know that something isn't right. Vicky and Nicola went off to find him. It was his afternoon off and he was about to go and play golf. I had a long discussion with him around the subject without ever mentioning it.

Later, when Nicola and I were sitting and talking about my experience of the day, I joked that I'd been touched up by about ten different people in less than a day. 'In my dreams,' I said.

I rang Ian and he was very calm. 'Don't worry,' he told me. 'It will be all right and we will take care of it.' We had a long discussion about whether we should tell Mum or not. We decided there was no point because it wouldn't do any good and would just worry her silly.

When we got back, I told some of the guys on the team

what had happened. Danny and Lloyd had known there was something wrong because I'd been so jittery and irrational. Everyone I spoke to seems to have had problems of their own or knows someone who has. I'm exhausted but I don't want to sleep. Tomorrow I'll see a breast consultant and should know one way or the other.

Tuesday, 10 October

Better news! It seems everything is okay. The specialist says he's 70 per cent sure it's not cancerous. 'The way it has developed and the speed of it makes me think it is not a problem,' he said. There was an option to put a needle into me, but the specialist thought that might create more problems because there was a risk of infection and that would be painful and might prevent me from racing. I can't do too much here because we're leaving for Sydney on Thursday. There's no point starting any treatment now. We decided it would be best to get it checked out when I get home. 'Make sure you do,' the consultant said. 'It's very important.' He was very up front and made sure that I know the seriousness of being careful.

I was half-reassured, but it is still there, niggling away at the back of my brain. Seventy per cent does not seem that much. I will try and lock it away until I get home but it is hard.

Wednesday, 11 October

While all this is going on, my hair colour is giving cause for concern, but at least I seem to speak to more team members because of it! I haven't been my true hair colour since I was thirteen. I'm naturally very dark but don't like it. My hair was nice at the Olympics but I decided I wanted some blonde high-lights put in. Nicola's uncle is a hairdresser, so she thinks she knows a lot about such things. She put the highlights in but that wasn't enough and we decided that I should be blonder. I ended up with a plastic bag on my head because, if it heats up, that apparently makes the colour work quicker. Then Nicola put the hair dryer on it. After about an hour of this my head was burning. I washed the dye out and then came the moment of truth. I raised my head and looked in the mirror. Panic! A carrot top was looking back at me. It was an absolute mess. My roots were white and then there was a repulsive yellow and orange mix. As soon as we could I went into town to buy some mahogany hair dye. I thought that would do the trick. According to the instructions it was meant to be on for twenty minutes but after five my hair had already gone a deep purple. By this point I was frantic. I washed the dye out and it was bright scarlet. Nicola came in to the bathroom while I was washing my hair and burst out laughing.

I got in the shower and turned it on full pelt. The curtains and the walls were instantly covered with this awful purple dye. I washed my hair nine times and after each one Nicola came in, peeked round the curtain and said, 'Nope, still red.' In the end I had to settle for pillar box red. It was not the colour I wanted to be seen with on television. Ian thinks it is very funny, Sian is horrified, James likes it and, luckily, Mum won't see it in the 800 metres because I'll have my helmet on.

To make matters worse, Nicola and I set off the fire alarm in our room. A light bulb exploded and the flames burnt the paper off the wall. The system for getting us out of the building failed. We are meant to be paired with non-disabled staff members who are meant to check that we are out of the building. All our

205

supposed rescuers were in another block, so Nicola and I had to go outside in our pyjamas. We were absolutely freezing. The people there wouldn't let us back in the room until everything was checked out, so we had to wait outside for about an hour. Dave Holding was there and he went off to make us a cup of tea. Eventually, we were allowed back into the building. Our room smelt of smoke and there was glass everywhere so we used the one next door. Nicola and I had to share a king-sized bed. We both slept right on the edges. It was odd really. We'd shared kit and most of our clothes in the past, so what was the problem with having to sleep in the same bed?

Thursday, 12 October

Moved from the Gold Coast to the Paralympic village today. The accreditation was at the airport which was much better than having it in the village as usual. The Gold Coast airport is a shed. We had to hang around for ages so I made a face out of a box. Pretty infantile but we thought it was funny. I cut two holes in it and put it on Nicola's head. Then I pulled her hair through the holes. We spent half an hour pushing round the airport while Nicola kept putting this box on her head. Nobody else thought it was remotely amusing, which probably says a lot about our sense of humour. I got some great pictures and I think we're probably quite sad.

Tuesday, 17 October

I've started going down with a cold. I can't believe it. After all the antibiotics I've been on because of my problems with the lumps I would have thought nothing could touch me!

Wednesday, 18 October

The opening ceremony. I felt okay through most of it. Got a bit wet but at least it is warm rain here. Took loads of Olbas oil to help clear my nose and did an interview with American television. The opening ceremony was more like a closing one. Everybody just piled in together instead of there being the normal organisation. I thought that was odd but it was an amazing atmosphere to be in. I think the best thing was seeing the athletes who were at a Paralympics for the first time – the emotion on their faces was amazing.

Thursday, 19 October

Spent most of the day asleep. Then I got up and did a light training session and felt better for it. Watched some of the races on television. Sarah Rowell, one of the sports scientists, came to our house. There are sixteen of us in here. I was sitting on the floor with my hooded top on and a duvet around me – just like a world-class athlete. I'll be okay for tomorrow, though. Went out with Dan at 6.30 p.m. because that's what time the race is. We pushed along the Louise Sauvage Pathway. That seemed a bit surreal as she's a good friend, but all the paths are named after Aussie athletes. We could see the track and the flame from the path. I talked to Dan about anything and everything. Twenty-four hours from now I'll be in there. I feel excited but calm.

Came home and had to call the doctor out for Karen. How much more! We now have a disease list on our wall in our kitchen because everybody in the house is picking up horrible illnesses. You name it, we've had it. Even Tom the cleaner is on the list because he's got a middle ear infection. There's a points system in place. You get one for seeing a physio, two for the doctor, three for going to the med centre and four for a scan. It's a bit childish but it's fun. We've also drawn a charity fund-raising-style thermometer on the wall and the more money we spend on treatment the more it goes up. It means everyone's going to the doctor and saying things like, 'So how much would an MRI cost then?'

The team spirit is so good here compared to Atlanta four years ago. We've borrowed a sheet from one of our cleaners and hung it on the wall. It's become the place where we write our thoughts of the day. We've got some fairly strict rules about what you can and can't say. You're not allowed to write anything about team management and you can't be seriously abusive about other athletes. It's all good-natured stuff, but someone from the team management wasn't happy when he saw the 'graffiti wall'. 'I hope you haven't stolen that,' he said. We said we hadn't, but I'm sure that in a village where there's 10,000 people, the odd sheet must go missing. 'I don't think it's funny,' he added. When he'd gone, one of the visually impaired athletes walked up to the set of rules and pulled it down. 'Sod him,' he said. Anything went after that.

Friday, 20 October

The day of the 800 metres final. I went down to breakfast and managed to keep it down until lunch. I sat with Stephen Herbert, Dan and Danny and everything seemed to be okay. Then I puked. Typical. I went down to track at 4 p.m. and Dan warmed up with me. Then it was time and we went to the call room, where you are held until the race. It was cold in there and we had to have all branding taped up again.

We were out on the track for what seemed like ages. I knew where Sian and James were in the stadium because of their flags. Once I'd found them I felt a lot better.

I'd thought of every possible race plan and had talked them through with Dan and Ian. I'm ringing Ian twice a day and spoke to him about an hour before the race. We didn't speak about the race then. I didn't want to be reminded of it.

It was a strange race. Cheri Blauwett didn't go off too hard and, although I hadn't planned to, I made a quick decision to hit the front. It worked and I kicked really hard at 400 metres. I used the television screens at each end of the stadium to see where everybody else was. That was a big help. I crossed the line first and felt very calm. I watched the re-run of the race on the screen. I went to find Sian and James, and Sian threw me her mobile phone so I could ring Ian. It's illegal to have phones on the track but I didn't care. It was 9 a.m. back home and Ian was in work. He'd been listening to it on the radio. Then he rang Mum and we all spoke. It was such a high.

Deep down I expect to win the 200 metres and 400 metres, but I was only fifty-fifty as regards the 800. At the medal ceremony Sian rang Mum on my mobile phone so that she and Dad could hear it live. When I saw Sian afterwards she had a sheepish grin on her face. 'I think you might have a big bill when you get home,' she said.

Saturday, 21 October

Day off. Already thinking about the next one now. No time to celebrate. Light training and sleep.

Sunday, 22 October

The 100 metres final. I knew that I was going to win. Don't know how or why, but I just had a strong feeling. Cheri Blauwett had a wide lane draw and I was in the middle. She's a great starter and I wasn't surprised to see her go off fast. Jessica Galli went with her. My start wasn't too good but the pick-up was. I got past Jessica and knew that I would reel Cheri in. I told myself not to panic. By 60 metres I was clear and the second gold medal was in the bag. I was a bit disappointed with the time. I'd expected to go a bit quicker, but who cares? I found Sian and James again. James is videoing all my races so he rewound it and I watched the replay by the side of the track. All you could hear was Sian's voice on the commentary getting higher and higher. In the 800 metres she had said, 'Why's she gone to the front? What's she doing? Get off the front.' Then on the 100 metre tape, she was saying, 'Why isn't she at the front? Get to the front, get to the front!' She was talking all the way through the race. I feel sorry for James but he is enjoying himself. He has never been to the Paralympics before but he's a huge sports fan.

Francesca Porcellato won a bronze. Earlier in the year I started experimenting by using a strap attached to my chair. I'd hold the other end of the strap in my mouth in an attempt to make myself more stable in the chair. It worked but I had to give it up because it made me gag. Francesca saw what I was doing and her husband Dino suggested she start doing the same. I like Francesca and I am really pleased for her. I watched the re-run of the race on the screen and was so happy to see her come home third. Francesca has just missed out so many times that it's great she's finally won a medal. She was so ecstatic afterwards it was as if she'd won the gold. She came up to me and said, 'Thanks for helping me,' which was nice. We did our victory laps together. That has actually been the most emotional part of the whole Games for me.

I can't celebrate too much but I'm really excited. I thought this was my weakest event, so that makes me feel comfortable. People are saying to me I'm going to win four golds, but I'm not thinking like that. The 100 metres was the longest 17 seconds I've ever endured but I'm in good shape.

Tuesday, 24 October

I got a fantastic lane draw for the 200 metres final. I was on the inside which meant I could see where everyone else was. Ideally, I like to be in two or three, but I'm not complaining. My plan was to pick everyone off as I went round.

The weather was cool and damp by the time the race came around, which was not the best, but I had a pre-race boost by not being sick beforehand. Maybe that was an omen because I had a great start and an equally good pick-up. By the time we came off the bend I had a decent lead. I came across the line and put my arm in the air. It felt great to have got a hat-trick but when I watched the video, I realised I looked miserable as sin. I stayed at the track to watch some of the athletics and begin to think that I can do four. The celebrations are on hold again, though, because there's another race coming.

Wednesday, 25 October

I went out for the evening with Sian and James and Rhidian and Rosie. Rhidian is a childhood friend of James's and Rosie is his Aussie girlfriend. They're coming to all my races which is nice of them. I wanted to get away from the village because it can get a bit claustrophobic. I also needed to release the pressure that is building up. Everybody is talking about winning a fourth gold. We went for a Chinese meal and I was very careful about what I ate. They had lucky crab. We thought that was quite funny. I hope it really is.

Thursday, 26 October

Rest day in the village. Didn't do much, apart from rest and think about the 400 metres tomorrow.

Friday, 27 October

I didn't feel good before the start of the 400 metres, both physically and mentally. I threw up and felt a bit jittery. I told Doc Campbell that I didn't want to be there. 'Typical athlete,' he said. I just want to go home. It seems like I've been away forever. To make matters worse, I got a bad lane draw, on the outside. I told myself to think about Gothenburg. If it had been on personal bests I'd have had a nice mid-lane draw, but they did it randomly. I had no choice but to go out hard. It would have been too risky to do anything else.

I gave it everything at the start but Madeline Nordlund came with me for the first 180 metres. I kept my head down and, coming off the bend, started to use the big screen to gauge where she was. When I got to the final bend I knew she wasn't with me. I crossed the line first and put my arm in the air again. Instead of elation, this time I just felt fatigue. I wanted to go and see Sian and James and collapse in a heap. I rang Ian from the international zone and then saw Doc Campbell. I went to the barrier and he gave me a big hug.

'How are you feeling?' he asked.

'Tired,' I said.

If I'd been honest I'd have said, 'Nothing.' It was strange. I just felt empty. It was a huge anticlimax. I've been preparing for this for so long and suddenly it is over and done. I had a stack of interviews to do and, though it was brilliant that there was so much media interest, I just wanted to forget about it all.

'You had me really worried there, Tanni,' Doc Campbell said. 'I was starting to panic.' Some of the team had thought that if Madeline went with me for the first 200 metres she might be able to stay with me.

I felt like I was going through the motions as I gave my interviews back at the hotel. Sian, James, Rhidian and Rosie were knocking back the champagne in the bar. 'You know, what I'd really like is a cup of coffee,' I said. They were on their third bottle by then and weren't going to let me get away with it. 'Don't be so boring,' said Sian, shoving a bottle of champagne into my hand. 'Drink this now.'

Sunday, 29 October

When Sian and I went out for the afternoon I bought a koala top – grey fleecy jumper with big ears on. One of the team dared me to wear it to the closing ceremony under my team kit. It was amazing to carry the Union Jack in to the closing ceremony.

I had never really thought about it before, but was asked this afternoon. I was lucky to walk past the British team and the response was incredible. It was a great party atmosphere and everybody was given these little sticks that glowed in the dark. Afterwards we went to a bar and Lloyd thrust a bottle of wine in my face to celebrate. I ended up swigging out of the bottle which shows how drunk I was! We ended up using the glow sticks as drink stirrers. Then we started putting them up our nostrils to make our noses turn a funny colour. I was absolutely pie-eyed and couldn't push straight. Dan made sure that I got home in one piece.

Monday, 30 October

Luckily, I don't have a hangover – that's the good thing about getting drunk very quickly. The bus was late arriving so we sat on the grass banking, helping ourselves to a pile of free ice creams. I'm leaving with mixed feelings. I am desperate to go but I am sad to be leaving the people I've become so close to in the past few weeks. I can't believe it's all over.

Chapter Eleven

The Blazer
Brigade

AFTER Sydney a tabloid newspaper rang me up and asked if I wanted to slag anyone off in the British team. I didn't and wouldn't ever dream of doing something like that. You don't see headlines saying *Golden Girl Tanni Grey Slams Establishment.* I don't throw stones. I think some people perceive me as a moaner because I speak my mind. But the fact of the matter is there are problems within athletics that need sorting out.

Take the return home from Sydney. It was a total mess that highlights the lack of planning that I find so irritating. They hadn't tagged the wheelchairs, so a lot of the athletes had to wait for ages at Heathrow while their frames were identified. When we knew there was a problem, Dan Saddler went to have a look. He came back down the aisle with a grim expression on his face. 'It's chaos out there,' he said, before trying to figure a way of getting everyone off the plane. In the end he gave me a piggyback because I had to go and do a television interview. As I went off down a corridor I saw one of the basketball guys sitting on the floor. Somebody must have carried him off, too. I asked, 'Are you all right?' He just shrugged his shoulders and rolled his eyes. It was such a shame and the annoying thing was we had spoken about it with the team management beforehand. We'd actually had a discussion and asked if we could all go through the gates at the airport together. They were shocked that some of us had been disappointed with what happened after Atlanta. But it wasn't any better coming home from Australia. The basketball player and some of the other guys were left sitting on the floor for over an hour. By the time they went through the gates the airport was deserted. After travelling for thirty-six hours that was not the best way to treat people. It is little wonder that some athletes think it is a them and us situation.

It's just a case of thinking about how athletes are treated. A few months after we came back from Sydney there was a reception for the Paralympic medal-winners at Buckingham Palace. It was the first time we'd ever had anything like that, so it was a sign that we were beginning to gain wider recognition. But the team management were pretty thoughtless and totally insensitive about the way they organised what should have been a great occasion. When we got there, the gold medallists were taken off into one room and the silver and bronze medallists were shepherded off somewhere else. It was as if they had no value at all. Unless you had a gold the BPA was not interested in you. Then, in the 'gold room', we had to stand in a horseshoe shape and this guy from the BPA said, 'The rest of you can stand where you want but Tanni has to be on the end because the Queen wants to meet her and all the cameras have to be on her.' There were nineteen other gold medallists in the room and I got a few looks from some of them. Most knew it wasn't my doing, but that sort of thing breeds resentment and makes people feel unwanted.

For some of the guys on the team, Sydney was their last Games. For others, it was the only time they'll make the team.

But it didn't matter to the team management. Their view is you have a higher value if you are contributing to the team in terms of medals. That's wrong because competing for Britain is a huge honour for everyone. So few people get to do it that, even if you don't win, you should be able to take something away from the experience. Unfortunately, that's not the case. After Sydney the team management were too busy falling over themselves to do things for me to worry about anyone else's feelings. Sport is not equitable but that does not mean everything else in the team can't be fair and even. That's the bit I get frustrated about and it comes down to man-management. The fact is, some of the people on the Great Britain team are awful at it.

Athletes are a strange breed. Why else would you go out training in the middle of November when it is –10 degrees and you could be sitting in the pub with your mates? And when it comes to competition time, you are not going to be at your most rational when you are being watched by 110,000 people. The team management need to understand that. After Sydney I found that people were either fawning all over me or implying I was deeply indebted to them. I just wished they could have been happy for me. When Danny Crates said, 'You're 100 metres was okay,' that meant so much more to me than the higher praise I got from some of the management. You have to treat athletes as decent human beings. There are a lot of pressures involved and you have to know how to get the best out of people. I know three athletes who have had nervous breakdowns and one who was suicidal because they had performed badly and felt they'd let everyone down. The governing body has to be closer to the athletes to understand what makes them tick. I'm lucky that Jenni, my coach, is a psychologist and she knows exactly how to get the best out of me. But if she treated her other athletes in exactly the same way it wouldn't work. We're human beings, not robots.

Part of the problem with those in charge of our sport is that they don't know where we fit in. Mainstream athletics have tried to integrate us but they are not sure how to treat us because we have spent years being segregated. That means a lot of coaches have no experience of disability and they get scared by it.

Having worked at UK Athletics I know that they are in a very difficult position. Disability athletics is a complete minefield and there are an awful lot of strong personalities in it who want to pull in different directions. Athletes, by nature, have forthright opinions and I don't envy UK Athletics in having to balance them all. But it is also true that a lot of Paralympic athletes don't feel they are wanted by the governing body. At best they feel we're tolerated by them. I don't think we've even reached that stage. It used to bother me more and it's forced me to rethink a lot of things. I always used to think disability athletics should be part of mainstream athletics. I thought they should take responsibility for us from the grass roots all the way to the top. Now I am not sure. I know Dave Moorcroft believes 100 per cent that we are part of mainstream athletics, but there are a lot of people who don't.

There are a lot of politics within UK Athletics between the performance and development sides. The performance people have to deliver Olympic gold and glory, and so have a very introverted view of their position within the sport. The development side is responsible for getting the kids in the first place and nurturing them. You can't have one side without the other but sometimes they do not work together as a team.

If I had my way, wheelchair racing would be part of cycling

rather than athletics. The cyclists understand our sport a lot better than athletics does. People at UK Athletics don't understand us because we don't fit into the neat little brackets that they have set up for athletics. You are meant to be either a sprinter, a middle distance runner or an endurance runner, but we do all events. I've been in the sport for sixteen years and I still have to explain to people at the governing body why I am able to do the 100 metres *and* the marathon. The answer is because every single person in wheelchair athletics does the same, but they don't take it on board.

The people in cycling instinctively have a lot better understanding of what we do. They know that it is possible to ride for a day and it all comes down to a sprint finish. I don't have to explain why tyres cost £180 or why I'm racing on tri-spokes instead of full discs. It's all to do with aerodynamics and how the wind moves over the spokes. I'm a member of a cycling club and I love it because so much is taken for granted and I don't have to answer all those repetitive questions that I do in athletics. Unfortunately, there's no chance of wheelchair racing becoming part of cycling because, internationally, we are considered part of the IAAF.

In an ideal world it would be nice to hand over all of wheelchair racing to the governing body and let them run the training camps, development, the kids, performance, the lot. But UK Athletics is not in a position to do that in terms of knowledge, manpower or money. Part of my reluctance to hand over control is the feeling that they just want to take the nice bits – things like the Paralympics and the World Championships. But the real underpinning work is development and if you don't get that right then you can kiss performance goodbye. At the moment there is no coaching qualification for wheelchair racing. There is in Australia and Canada but we are lagging behind. It is being worked on now but the coaching structure hasn't been changed for ten years.

It is not just the governing body that needs to change its attitude. When I have helped out at Wheelchair Racing Association weekends, I have found a lot of thirteen-year-olds have absolutely no independence at all. They don't know how to brush their teeth or have a shower because somebody else has always done that for them. Some of that comes from home and some of it comes from school where they have not been encouraged to fend for themselves. They might come to a flight of steps and it would never occur to them to get out and pull their chairs up after them. On one occasion Sian was helping out and a boy refused to comb his hair. 'My mum always does it for me,' he said.

'Well I'm not your mum and I'm not doing it,' she said.

'But I've never done it before.'

He was a spoilt brat but it wasn't really his fault. He was someone who'd got low expectations because of the way he had been brought up and educated.

It's difficult for disabled kids in mainstream schools and also for the PE teachers who don't have specialist training in disability sport. But we need to decide how seriously we want to take it and implement development programmes to get them through. It is easy to target disabled kids because there are not many of them. Some schools do an amazing job, but a lot of kids have a concept of integration that stems from the Dark Ages.

Another thing that happened post Sydney was I had lots of people asking me where they could get application forms for the Paralympics. I had to tell them it doesn't work like that. But

Receiving the OBE – April, 2000.

Launching the 'Tanni Grey' lifeboat – one of the most emotional moments in my life.

The 'Tanni Grey' lifeboat in action – the fastest class of boat in the RNLI fleet.

My room-mate Nicola in a mask I artistically made for her – Gold Coast, 2000.

After a long night of celebration at the Sydney Games closing ceremony.

Sian and James at their patriotic best!

Winning the 800m – a defining image of my Games in Sydney.

Sydney 2000 – overcoming my nerves to win gold.

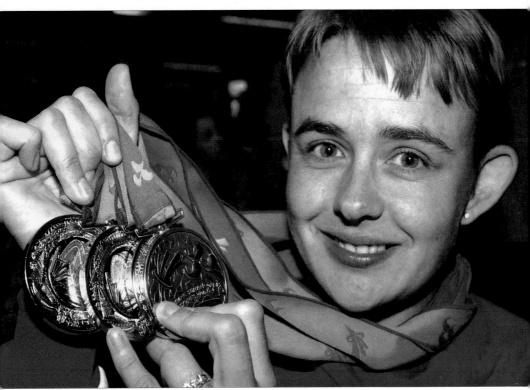

A jubilant arrival back at Heathrow.

Nikki Rollason presents me with the *Sunday Times* Sportswoman of the Year award.

Fashion shoot for the *Daily Mail.*

BBC Sports Personality of the Year 2000 – together with Steve Redgrave, who won, and Denise Lewis, who was second.

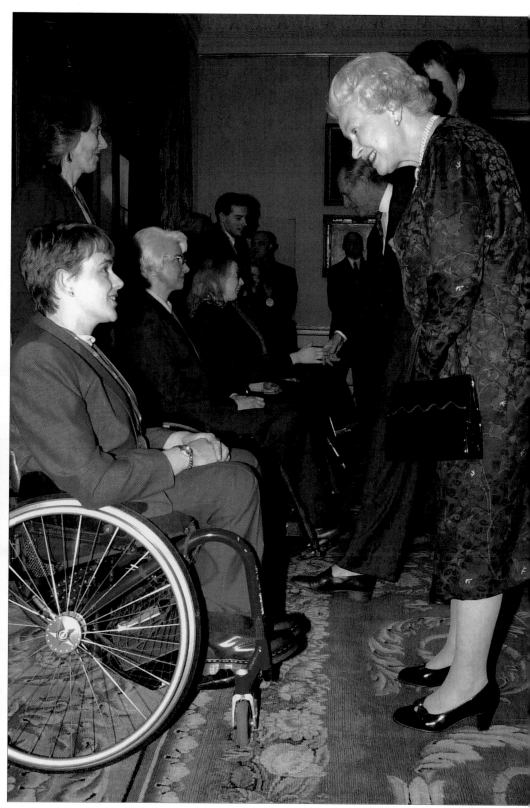

Buckingham Palace reception for the victorious Paralympic team.

Receiving my London Marathon trophy from the PM in 2001.

Ian (*right but half-hidden*) and Martin, my agent, dressed as penguins at the Laureus Sports Gala Awards in Monaco, 2001.

Winning the London Marathon in 2001, with the BBC camera strapped to my helmet.

that is another perception we have to change. We need to make people realise that the Paralympics are about élite sport. Some athletes in the squad have been able to get away with not being élite because certain sections of the Paralympics are not as well developed as others. Disability sport was set up with the intention of making it fair, but sport isn't fair and it shouldn't be. If it was, we'd all come across the line together holding hands.

Occasionally, when I've been frustrated, I have felt that wheelchair racing should push to become a full Olympic event and stuff everyone else. In 1999 I thought we should try as hard as we could to get full medal status for the women's 800 metres and the men's 1500 metres. But that feeling didn't last for long and I now think we should put all our energy into developing the Paralympics. It's an amazing event but it needs refining. There are too many classes and they need cutting down. We need to make sure people with severe disabilities are not excluded but not to the extent where it is not a true competition. The Paralympics is meant to be the stage for the best disabled athletes in the world. It is not a development competition. If there aren't enough people competing then the event shouldn't be on. That's where the development work comes in. You don't just go down the street and find a thrower with a certain type of disability. And the patterns in some disability groups are changing because of improved medical treatment and screening. For example, these days there are fewer kids with spina bifida because of the testing available and because women have the choice whether to go through with the pregnancy or not. Now we are looking at different types of people coming through the ranks.

We have to get development right because in the next ten years we are going to find ourselves under increasing threat from other countries. For instance, civil war is going to have a huge impact on wheelchair athletics. Places such as Kosovo now have a huge number of amputees and they are going to beat everybody out of sight in time. It's the same in some of the African countries. At the moment we are not a third world sport because the equipment is too expensive but that is changing. I am not suggesting we start ambulance chasing in this country, but we need to monitor our kids, encourage them and give them a structured coaching programme.

Lottery funding has changed so much for athletes. Now you have to perform because your future depends on it. The money has enabled us to do so much more but some athletes struggle with the accountability. Now, at the start of each year, you have to state the targets that you are going to reach, whether they be times, distances or medals. At the start of 2000 I said I would reach specific times and win one or two golds and two silvers at the Paralympics. Now we have some good young guys in Britain who should make it to the 2008 Paralympics as well as Athens in 2004. But unless we can plot what times they should be doing and when, they are not going to get there. It's no good them sitting back and thinking, oh we've got another seven years. Ian and I are happy working within a fairly rigid structure, but some younger athletes have found it hard. They just pluck numbers out of the air.

I became a member of the Lottery Council in 1998. The idea of the council is to have a group of impartial people with expertise in various fields who can ensure that government money is being spent in the right way. Sometimes it is not, but there are a lot of talented people there. The UK Sport Lottery Unit is run by Liz Nicholl, who came from netball and has an athlete-centred approach. She is very caring, astute and heavily into planning. She has revolutionised Lottery funding by giving guarantees to sport that they will have funding if they perform. She is making sure athletes are treated right and that is encouraging.

I think I would be good at man-management and treating individuals as they should be treated. That's why I can see myself getting involved in coaching in the future. My hobby at the moment is helping people at the weekends or getting them to take up the sport. We have loads of people who come to our house to use the treadmill we've got in the garage, and I do my best to teach them how to push. Ian and I both think this is an amazing sport to be part of and we want other people to enjoy it as much as we do. We are passionate about it and find it difficult to walk away. That's why the attitudes of some of those in authority grate so much.

Another issue that needs addressing in disability athletics is the sheer number of governing bodies. There are far too many groups out there trying to provide sport for disabled people. It means it's a very complicated picture for anybody just getting involved in sport. And the different governing bodies don't communicate with each other. Athletics doesn't talk to swimming and vice versa. In wheelchair racing alone there is a string of organisations who all feel they are my governing body. There's the British Wheelchair Sport Foundation, the British Wheelchair Sport Association, the Wheelchair Racing Association, the BPA Athletic Federation, the BPA, UK Athletics, UK Sport, etc. It just gets too confusing and muddled. It would be the best thing for the sport if we got rid of all the different disability governing bodies. That won't happen because people don't want to give away their control. People are too concerned with protecting their own interests.

There needs to be a better dialogue between the athletes and those governing them. It's easy for some of the people in the governing body to consider me a stroppy individual because I get irritated by the fact the things we are fighting for haven't changed in twelve years. It's mainly a question of man-management and wanting to have an equal footing with mainstream athletics. This year there was a long debate about whether we would be allowed to wear British kit. We're part of UK Athletics and have Lottery funding, yet we don't have the right to have the kit that the mainstream athletes have. That might seem a fairly minor point but we are proud to represent Britain so we should be allowed to wear the kit.

Everyone always blames someone else. If an athlete asks the governing body a tough question, they immediately blame the Lottery people, because they are the faceless individuals who work in the Sports Council and are easiest to blame.

I think sometimes they think they are protecting us. This year I asked for my name to be put on the out of competition doping register. That means the testers can turn up at my house at any time of the day asking for a sample. I wanted to be on it because I think we should be dealt with in the same way as the mainstream athletes. But UK Sport put just five names on the register as a token gesture. They did that without discussing the issue with us. I don't believe there is any disabled British athlete who is on steroids. Half of them don't know what they are and the other half couldn't afford them anyway. But we are Lottery funded so we should be treated in the same way as anyone else. If you are taking money from the government, you should be clean and able to prove it. Three-quarters of the athletes in the squad couldn't care less if they are on the register or not. But our governing bodies should consult us. If I get caught doping, it's me who loses my Lottery funding and everything. But the people making these decisions for us don't talk to us. In trying to protect us they are actually underestimating us.

Integration has gone too slowly in Britain. I used to think we would be so much better off as athletes if we were included within the governing body but I don't think we are. I thought the move would have been a lot more positive than it has turned out. I think that is largely due to the attitudes towards the disabled. But that is changing and the condescending attitude to our sport is diminishing. Ten years ago they might have thought we were messing about, but now they realise we are training as hard as non-disabled athletes. I don't have a problem if coaches don't want to coach disabled athletes. You can't force it on people and everyone has their own preferences – some only coach women, some only coach 200 metres, etc. But we do need more coaches because, at the moment, the knowledge is coming just from the athletes themselves.

In an ideal world it would be so much easier if we were fully integrated and not kept separate. I find it very useful to train with non-disabled people and I'd rather be a member of a mainstream sports club than a disabled one. I can't see why, if there is a sprinters' training weekend, we can't have Olympic and Paralympic athletes together. My friend Danny Crates is an arm amputee and he trains with Donna Fraser. They post similar times on the track and they benefit from training with each other. Maybe a female cerebral palsy runner would fit in with a non-disabled Under-19 runner. The mainstream athletes would not have a problem with it themselves. A few might do but you'll get the odd bigot wherever you go. At Cardiff we always trained with the runners. Everyone just wants good training partners and it shouldn't matter whether you are disabled or not. It just comes down to finding someone of a similar standard in terms of times. That is not going to happen, though, because there is not the political will to make it reality.

I also don't think there's any problem with non-disabled people competing in wheelchairs. In this country there's only Dan Saddler who does and that's because he's grown up around the sport. His dad is Chas Saddler who helped fix my puncture in my first London Marathon. But when I go into schools the first things kids say is, 'Give us a go in your wheelchair.' They think it's exciting. People don't compete because of the stigma that is attached to wheelchairs and because they don't know they can. But what's the difference between Dan and Ian? Nothing. Our sport is fast and exciting so it should be open to all. Chairs are like bikes. Racing them is a thrill so why should it be restricted to the disabled? There's as much skill, technique and power needed to race wheelchairs as there is bikes. Obviously, they'd need to go in the right class to avoid having an unfair advantage. I am not suggesting we should go out and actively seek non-disabled athletes to start wheelchair racing, although if more did it that would make the sport sexier. Our priority should be giving our disabled athletes the best chance to fulfil their potential.

I should point out that there is a difference between officials in athletics and those in governance. Every single official I have ever met has been a nice person. Some are very strict, John Tanner for instance, but they give up a huge amount of time for the love of the sport. Some people think they make a lot of money but they don't. We are totally dependent on these volunteers. I had to organise a budget for one competition and part of my job was to sort out the hotel accommodation and expenses. I told the officials that they could have what they wanted from the menu and a reasonable amount of drinks. The next day a guy came to me and was incredibly apologetic. 'I had a pint of beer and put it on the room bill by mistake,' he said.

'Don't worry about it,' I said. 'If you'd drunk the mini-bar dry that might be different.'

He wouldn't accept it, though, and gave me the two quid. That's the sort of attitude that keeps the sport going. These people are amazing. They get no recognition but, without them, we wouldn't be able to carry on. When athletes slag off officials they actually mean the people in the governing body. It's a shame because their anger is not directed at the officials, but they get very upset about it.

My experience of the governing body is that it can be like banging your head against a brick wall. I don't think they make the best use of the expertise that exists within the sport, although I wouldn't want to get involved myself. There is too much politics involved and I would find it incredibly frustrating. But I also know that I will never be able to completely walk away. If I was to work with them I would need to believe it was worth investing my time. At the moment I don't think I do.

Chapter Twelve

Aim High Even if You Hit a Cabbage

WHEN I was a little girl, Dubby Jones, my grandfather, used to say to me, 'Aim high even if you hit a cabbage.' He meant that you should set your sights high even if you end up on the floor. If you suffer setbacks or disappointments, you should pick yourself up, focus on new goals and try again. It doesn't matter where you end up as long as you are trying. That saying of his has become my motto. I don't think anything I've done has ever ended in failure. I don't mean that to sound arrogant but, to me, you can't fail if you try. Some people might say I've failed at certain things, but I just think they have not turned out as I'd hoped. I have a fatalistic outlook on life. Whatever will be will be. That is why I don't get really depressed after losing races. It's nothing to do with having a disability, it is just my personality. I've always been determined and ambitious. If I hadn't been an athlete, I am sure I would have put as much passion and energy into doing something else. It's much better to give it your all – then, if something doesn't go to plan, you know that you have kept to your side of the bargain.

Sydney changed my life in a way Barcelona in 1992 didn't. From the moment I stepped off the plane at Heathrow, things would never be the same again. The amount of media coverage was immense. There were television crews waiting when we landed. When I met up with Mum and Dad at Newcastle Airport, they showed me the press cuttings and told me how I'd been on the Nine O'Clock News. We'd never had this sort of coverage before. As I walked through the airport, lots of people came up to me to shake my hand and congratulate me. It was an amazingly positive reception.

I think the Olympics had generated a feel-good factor that carried over to the Paralympics. It was also important that the Games were so well organised. Suddenly, I was in constant demand. Requests for me to do things started coming in immediately. It was never-ending. One day I'd be in Redcar, the next I'd be in Cardiff and the next I'd be in London.

One thing I did soon after I got home was attend a fashion shoot in London for the *Daily Mail*. Lee Pearson, an equestrian who won three golds, was there along with a few other Paralympians. I was given a gorgeous red velvet dress to wear, but it didn't fit, so they held it together at the back with bulldog clips. Then they gave me a pair of £600 Jimmy Chu high-heeled shoes. My feet are quite wide so I couldn't get them on. In the end I wore my trainers and they placed these shoes in front of me, peaking out from beneath the dress, so it looked as if I was wearing them. They had a guy there to put my make-up on. I hadn't looked in the mirror so we did the shoot and then I had to rush home.

'Do you want me to take your make-up off?' said this guy.

'No, I'll be all right,' I said.

As I went through the airport I started to attract a lot of attention. I thought, this is nice, everybody recognises me. Then I went to the loo and caught my reflection in the mirror. I had bright red lipstick and glittery gold make-up all over my cheeks and forehead. No wonder everyone had been staring.

I didn't have any competitions to prepare for in the aftermath of Sydney, but found myself working seven days a week. One day it would be the *Daily Mail* and the next I'd be speaking at the Welsh Assembly. From meeting the Mayor of Birmingham to visiting schools, the variety of things I was being asked to do was incredible. The only trouble was the extra pressure that it put on me. I got the all clear from the breast clinic when I got back, but other things began to take their toll. I had three days off in nine months after Sydney and, although I enjoyed the things I was doing, I came close to burning myself out. I was mentally and physically drained. I usually like being busy and travelling around, but it got to the stage where I didn't want to go anywhere. I feel guilty saying no to people, though, so I carried on and I got more and more bogged down with it. I was spending two nights a week at home if I was lucky. That was difficult because it meant I didn't get to see Ian. It's been hard on Ian, too, because I get to do all the nice stuff. We had a lot of problems finding a date to move house and the one we eventually landed on ended up clashing with the Welsh Sports Personality of the Year. So I went off to a plush ceremony and Ian had to move house. He doesn't complain and we both know this is the way it has to be, but that doesn't make it any easier.

Recently I have been spending more time with Ian; it has been wonderful and we agreed that it would be the perfect time to start a family. For so long our priorities have been based around competing and up until now I felt that we weren't ready. I think Sydney changed those ideas for me. Part of it has to do with my age, but also for the first time I didn't definitely know that I was going to compete in the next Games.

Many people say that having a family will change our lives in terms of our sporting ambitions. It is true that I have seen dedicated athletes who have suddenly decided they no longer wish to compete. On the other hand, I have seen athletes train and compete virtually all the way through motherhood. Until it happens to me I can't say how I'll feel. It is something that Ian and I are both enormously looking forward to, and we will decide what is best for us as a family when the time comes.

The fact I'll be in a wheelchair and have a young child running around doesn't worry me at all. Ian's sister, Faith, has a daughter, Georgia, and we get on really well. And I've been to stay with Ric Cassell, who is a wheelchair-user, and his kids recognise that he can't go chasing after them, so they don't bother running away. They understand a lot about having a parent in a wheelchair. My main concern is the pregnancy – I'm not into pain and the bits you see on television look incredibly gruesome. Being pregnant and being in a wheelchair will also pose some problems when it comes to moving about. The thought of things like transferring myself from my wheelchair to the sofa and how I'll cope getting my chair in and out of the car when I'm really fat are quite scary.

Ian and I have talked about what we would do if we had a child with a disability. I think a lot of the things I have been through would be helpful and having me as a mum might make some things easier. Lots of people ask me how I'd feel if my child was disabled and the honest answer is I don't know. I can't answer that until it happens. What I do know is Ian will be a more patient parent than I will. People probably think I'm more tolerant than him because he has a sharp sense of humour and can come across as a bit cynical, even though he's not, but it's actually the other way round. He's far more patient with Georgia than I am. My plan is to earn enough money for Ian to be able to retire and look after our children!

People keep asking me what I'm going to do when I retire. I told one person my ambition was to become the Eurovision Song Contest host. It was a joke but I was fed up with being asked the question because I plan to keep competing for a long time yet. I don't think I have reached my peak and I don't think I will until I am in my mid-thirties. It takes a long time to develop your strength, technique and race tactics and I honestly think the Paralympics in Athens in 2004 could be when I am at my best. It's going to be very hard to win another four gold medals, though, because of the increasing competition. Over the next few years the Americans will develop in leaps and bounds. They have a bunch of teenagers who are going to be a major threat. Some of the African and eastern bloc nations will also begin to make an impact because of the structures they now have in place and the fact they see disability sport as a really positive form of rehabilitation.

It's not that we are lagging behind in Britain. We started the whole thing off and led the way for years, but other countries have now caught us up. The face of the sport is changing. Australia are one of the strongest countries at the moment but I think they may have trouble sustaining their success. They have a population of only 17 million and get less funding than we do. The thing they have going for them is the fact they are very efficient and have some excellent programmes in place to develop athletes. They also recognise the importance of forward planning and many of those who did so well in Sydney had been developmental athletes in Atlanta four years earlier.

Another thing the Aussies did so well was the massive schools programme they ran two years before the Paralympics. Athletes would go into schools and there was a video and a workbook tied into the curriculum focusing on the Paralympics, athletes and disability. Targeting children was a sensible approach because the Olympics and Paralympics are supposed to be about changing cultural and societal behaviour. The fact they sold a million tickets suggests they got it right. I think it is vitally important to teach kids about disability and disability sport. What I have found so encouraging is that, when I have gone into schools since Sydney, the children are incredibly positive about the Paralympics. Five years ago they wouldn't have had a clue what they were. Now they are genuinely interested. I went to the school where Ric's children go and every single child asked me a different question about the Games. Why do you have a number on your knees? What happens if you have to share a room with someone you hate? What was the food like? They all knew the difference between the Olympics and Paralympics. If future generations are interested then the future is bright. If you asked kids in a mainstream school what they wanted to do, most would probably say they wanted to be a footballer rather than going to the Olympics. If you asked disabled kids the same question, you'd get a high percentage saying they wanted to go to the Paralympics. We have to foster their interest and encourage them. Going into schools is one of the things I enjoy most. The kids are so honest. They'll ask anything they like, whereas adults will skirt around issues. I think we can learn a lot from the kids. If everybody was as open about disability as they are, it would be better for us all.

I don't think I can go on competing at the top level much past my mid-thirties. Sooner or later the team selectors will drop me from the squad or I will retire. It's just a question of which comes first. When one or the other happens I will take a break and go and try something different. I will be doing some broadcasting for the BBC this winter and maybe I will do more media work; or perhaps I'll become more actively involved with coaching. Whatever happens, I cannot imagine giving up racing altogether. A lot of older women in the sport take a couple of months out and then come back and compete for a bit. I may do that, which means I could be around for a long time yet!

I will definitely stop before I get too injured. Being an athlete is a case of swings and roundabouts. I'm much healthier as a disabled person because I'm fit, but the downside is I'm knackered! The endless training and competing takes its toll. Blisters are not as much of a problem as some people might think, but injured shoulders, elbows and fingers are. Wheelchair racing is all about technique and the angle at which you hold your shoulders, elbows and wrists. The most important part of the wheel is the bottom of the rim between four and eight o'clock. That's where you get the speed from. You have to be strong but you also need hand speed. You have to get your wrists positioned correctly and turn them as you push round. You also need good shoulder mobility, so you can lift them high enough to punch downwards. My wrists aren't too bad, but my shoulder and elbow joints have worn down. My shoulders click a lot and they ache in winter. I also get a dull ache in my left elbow and my finger joints are a mess. It's part and parcel of being an athlete, just as a footballer might end up with bad knees. But it was one of the things we thought about when we moved house. We knew we needed somewhere that was going to be accessible for us when we are older and decrepit!

I am trying not to think too far ahead. I began concentrating

on Sydney a long time beforehand, but I can't even contemplate
Athens at the moment. In 2002 we have the Europeans, World
Championships and the Commonwealth Games. I am putting
my energy into thinking about those. With the Commonwealth
Games being held in Manchester it is important for me to do
well, but I know it will be very hard. It's an open event, so I'll
be up against T4s and it will effectively be the Olympic final
mark two. Having seen how the Aussies reacted to competing
in front of their home crowd, I think it will be amazing to race
in Manchester next year. The Commonwealth Games will be
the closest I ever get to experiencing what the Aussies had in
Sydney. I also know how valuable a major games can be in terms
of urban regeneration and presenting a positive profile. I don't
think we'd have been ready to hold the Paralympics in 2000 but
I think we would now, in terms of attitude if not facilities.

If I am to do well in Manchester, I cannot allow my training
to suffer because of all the other things that I have taken on
since Sydney. That means training six days a week. I usually
spend an hour in the gym doing bench presses, pull-ups, dips
and tricep work. Then I'll do lots of rehabilitation exercises for
my shoulders and some drills intended to strengthen my back
muscles which are fairly weak. I don't have good stomach
muscles so I try to do some half sit-ups, which is actually just a
lot of flapping around on the floor and makes Ian laugh. I then
lie on my front and try to raise my head and shoulders up. Ian
can do that but my head only gets about an inch off the floor.
In the winter I'll play basketball and train with the local team.
We do plenty of resistance work where someone pulls another
person for a length-and-a-half of the gym and then lets go. I
used to play in competitive games too, but stopped because of
the danger to my hands. The guys were great and wouldn't tackle

me very hard because they knew my hands were my livelihood, but I didn't think it was worth the risk in the end. I'll also do three weight-training sessions a week and put in the miles on the road and the treadmill. It's a gruelling regime but it's one I enjoy and it has paid off so far.

I thought the interest in me would die down after Sydney. But the furore that followed the ramp business at the BBC Sports Personality of the Year ensured things kept coming in. If I'd just got third place and there had been no 'incident', people would have forgotten about it by now. But, ironically, an oversight by the BBC has done wonders for the profile of disability sport.

It all started when Sian rang me. 'You've made the advert for BBC Sports Personality,' she said. I was amazed and found the fact I was on the trailer quite exciting. There were various different trailers and I was featured on some more than others. That meant a lot of calls from Sian and Mum to discuss why they'd shown that particular version that night. It was an exciting time because I'd dreamed about being a winner since I'd started watching the programme as a young girl. Then, three days before the show went out, I knew that I'd made the top six. Martin thought I had a reasonable chance of winning the Helen Rollason special award, but I thought that would go to the Paralympic team as a whole.

There was no rehearsal and we had to be in our seats forty-five minutes before the start. I was sitting with the Paralympic team but I was late into the studio because I'd been outside talking like I usually am. I ended up on the second row, but the floor manager wasn't happy and he made two other athletes move so that I could be on the front row. They got a bit stroppy. I thought, this is great for team spirit. I'm very conscious that some of the people in the team think, oh, bloody hell, it's her again, old Moanyhead. I can understand that because if it was someone else who was always getting the attention, I'd feel that way too. I'd been to Sports Personality lots of times, but it's only recently that I've graduated to the level where they let you bring someone with you. It takes about ten years. Ian doesn't like that sort of thing so Martin came with me. It's quite a surreal occasion. One year I was sitting next to Mika Hakkinen. He asked me what I did. I told him and he said, 'Oh, that's nice. I'm a racing driver.' I thought, yeah, I know! It's very hard not to sit there and star spot.

The thing that annoyed me most about that night was not the ramp, as most people might imagine, but the way they did the interview with me when I got the Helen Rollason award. Two other Paralympians, Lee Pearson and Dave Roberts, a swimmer, were sitting on a sofa on a podium and I was in my chair on the floor. It meant I was lower down, looking up at them and Clare Balding, who was doing the interview. I thought, the BBC are better than this. During a lot of interviews I choose to stay in my wheelchair because there's a morbid curiosity in watching disabled people trying to transfer themselves and I don't like to satisfy that. I don't mind scrambling across the floor but I don't want to make people feel uneasy.

When they announced I was the winner of Helen's award I didn't feel very comfortable. It was billed as an award for someone who had overcome adversity and I don't think that applies to me. If it had been the Helen Rollason Award for anything else, it would have been amazing to win it because I thought so much of her as a person. I keep working hard at telling people that I'm not struggling against the odds but I can't escape it. Disability does not fit into adversity but they are always linked together. In Sydney the Paralympics had been marketed as a sporting event, pure and simple. Nobody asked, 'What have you had to overcome in your disability?' It was, 'What have you had to overcome as an athlete.' It was a refreshing approach.

Clare Balding wasn't terribly happy with the interview either and apologised to me afterwards. She was worried because she thought I wanted to say something, but I didn't. I couldn't possibly sum up what I thought of Helen in just a few words. If I'd started even to attempt to do so then I would have got very emotional and ended up crying. And I didn't think it would have been very useful for Nikki, Helen's daughter, to see someone else getting so upset over her mum. I have tried to tell her since what I thought about Helen, but a live television interview was not the place. I still think about Helen a lot and when I do it makes me cry. I just think, why did it have to happen to someone so nice when there are plenty of horrible people in the world? Afterwards Sian said that I looked totally miserable when they gave me her award, but it was just so difficult to sum up anything about Helen in a single sound bite – Hard-working, bloody-minded, fighting the system? Without having the time to think it through in my head I wouldn't have been able to do it justice, so I didn't say anything.

Having got Helen's award, I thought that would be that. A lot of thoughts were running through my head, about Helen and about how poorly they had set up the interview. Then they came to the top three awards. And they read out my name. I was amazed. Helen's award made sense because it pigeonholed me into the adversity category, but getting third place in the main award was a complete surprise. If I'd looked unhappy because of all the conflicting emotions I was feeling when I got Helen's trophy, this time I was jubilant. When I realised there was no ramp it honestly didn't bother me. My main gripe was that I was sitting with a group of swimmers whom I didn't know, so I didn't really have anyone to share it with. I did think it was a bit odd when Steve Redgrave and Denise Lewis got first and second place and they came down and stood on the stage, while I was stuck away at one side, but I was just very happy.

It was other people who were more upset about it than I was and made me realise there was a problem. At the post-awards party Peter Salmon, the head of sport, came up to me and apologised. 'We've had a lot of phone calls,' he said. Martin suggested that we issue a joint statement with the BBC and we did that. We thought that was the conciliatory thing to do. I thought it would blow over, but people still talk to me about it even now. It was no big deal as far as my personal feelings were concerned, but it was a big deal in terms of encouraging a better understanding of disability.

Getting awards is nice. It's the icing on the cake. It was nice to think some people thought I was a more worthy winner than someone with as high a profile as David Beckham, who was one of the others on the short list. Sian brought me back down to earth immediately, though, when she rang me and joked, 'Yeah, but you have to remember everyone hates Beckham.'

Since Sydney the awards have kept coming. In 2001, I received six new honorary degrees. They are nice because they are a different level of recognition. I'd already got doctorates from Staffordshire, Manchester Metropolitan, Southampton and St Mary's College, Surrey, plus a master's degree from Lough-borough. This year I've had doctorates from the University of Wales Institute Cardiff, Swansea, Loughborough, Ripon College and Leeds Metropolitan. I've also had the Chancellor's Medal from the University of Glamorgan. That's not a bad haul.

In May I received another honour when I was voted on to the Laureus World Sports Academy. That is a new group of sportsmen and women, including the likes of Pele, Michael Jordan, Seve Ballesteros and Martina Navratilova. The idea is to help the Sport for Good Foundation which aims to tackle social issues through sport. It's an honour to be part of the academy and Ian, Martin and I travelled to Monte Carlo in May where I was to be inducted at the Laureus Sports Awards. It was an incredibly glitzy ceremony attended by film stars and sporting legends but, to be honest, it was not my cup of tea. It was far too glamorous and there were way too many middle-aged men with young blonde girlfriends. It wasn't the real world. Ian went to the hotel gym one day and found himself on the walking machine next to Ringo Starr, while Boris Becker paraded up and down outside rehearsing his speech for the ceremony. When the time came to leave the hotel for the venue, the Mercedes that was picking us up could not stop immediately outside because there was another car parked there. It meant we had to walk all of five yards, but the girl from the hotel wouldn't let us. She kept apologising profusely and hurried off to get someone to move the parked car. It was strange.

Then, as we were going into the hall where the awards ceremony was taking place, Catherine Zeta Jones turned around and saw me. I'd never met her before, but she came over and said, 'Hello, how are you?' I thought that was sweet. Maybe it was because we're both Welsh. Then her husband came over and said, 'Hi, I'm Michael.' We acted very cool but once they had gone, we burst out laughing. I couldn't believe we'd just met Michael Douglas. If that was surreal, it got more so as the night progressed. Martina Navratilova came over to me at one point and congratulated me for joining the academy. We then sat there discussing Jennifer Capriati's shoes. She had won the Comeback of the Year Award.

'She could hardly walk in those high heels,' Martina said.

'I don't wear high heels,' I said and pulled up my dress to show her my trusty purple Docs.

'That's brilliant,' she said. 'And they match your dress.'

She proceeded to talk about how she'd chosen a pair of comfortable flat shoes that she could run a marathon in. When I went back to my seat, Ian said, 'Where've you been?'

'Oh, talking shoes with Martina,' I said.

He laughed. Although I don't idolise people, I still get a little bit star struck. I think it would be a shame to lose that. They are real people but they are still stars. I tried out my French on Miguel Indurain, the famous cyclist, and had a quick chat with Ilie Nastase. Then I caused mayhem on the escalators. To get off I had to lean back and do a little wheelie to pop my wheels over the top. But everybody was pushing up from behind and I got jammed. It was like a bottle and cork effect after that. Bobby Charlton was panicking like hell and Martin grabbed me round the neck. When we managed to get off I ended up being carried up another flight of stairs by Steve Redgrave. And then Martin and I went round the back where we saw the Miami Dolphin cheerleaders wearing next to nothing and proving their flexibility. We then had a very philosophical discussion about how many of them had breast implants. It was a bizarre evening!

Monte Carlo is too flash for me and even if I had the money, I wouldn't want to live there. I'd been there before in 1993 when I was supporting the Manchester Olympic bid and I remember having a tiny meal in a restaurant along with Chris Boardman, Steve Redgrave and Adrian Moorhouse and the bill coming to £180 a head. A Coke on room service was £8. I missed the final bid because I had to fly to Germany to compete. I was sitting in the airport waiting for my flight when I met an Aussie, complete with a hat with corks on. We decided to find a television to watch the announcement and got drunk together. When they said Sydney had won he started screaming and jumping around the chairs. I thought that was a great way to see the outcome and it suited me better than sitting in some ridiculously fancy restaurant.

But the positive thing about being a member of the World Sports Academy is that I will get the opportunity to make a difference. Each academy member has to do his bit, whether it be by raising the profile of the Sport for Good Foundation, raising money or visiting projects. That is exciting and I am glad to be a part of such an illustrious group. To think that I am rubbing shoulders with some of the all-time greats in sport shows how attitudes are changing. A few years ago a disabled athlete would never have been involved in something so high profile as that.

It's been a long road. The child once taunted with the nickname 'Limpy Legs' has come a long way. The teenaged girl so impressed by seeing the Great Britain basketball team on television has seen her dreams realised. Now I am in my thirties and eagerly anticipating the future. Sydney has taken Paralympics to a new level. Now we need to build on it. Awareness of disability issues is rising and the barriers are being broken down. If I have played a small part in that, then that is something I can be proud of. I did not set out with a mission to do so but things have happened along the way. I hope I make people feel comfortable about the idea of disability sport because I am not too confrontational. When I stop racing, others will follow. When that happens I hope people will remember me as a good athlete and a nice person. That's the best I can hope for. But there are still goals to set and races to be won. I am still ambitious and so I'll continue aiming high and trying to miss those cabbages.

Index